John Montague : Collected Poems

# JOHN
# MONTAGUE

WAKE FOREST UNIVERSITY PRESS

# COLLECTED
# POEMS

First U.S. edition published 1995.
Published in association
with The Gallery Press,
Loughcrew, Oldcastle,
Co. Meath, Ireland.
For a summary of
previous publications, see the
bibliographical
note in the back. For permission,
required to reprint
or broadcast more than several
lines, write to
Wake Forest University Press,
PO box 7333,
Winston-Salem, NC 27109.
Designed by Richard Eckersley.
Set in Adobe Minion.
Printed in Ireland.
ISBN 0-916390-68-3
(in paper covers)
ISBN 0-916390-69-1
(cloth binding )
LC card no. 95-61011

ACKNOWLEDGMENTS: I wish to thank my
diligent and dedicated editors — Peter Fallon
and Dillon Johnston — Candide Jones of
Wake Forest University Press, and Elizabeth,
my eagle-eyed companion. — J. M.

*for my children*
*for my friends*

# CONTENTS

# 1

# 2

**Forms of Exile** (1958) & **Poisoned Lands** (1961, 1977)  187

# 3

**Time in Armagh** (1993)  329

John Montague : Collected Poems

# 1

# THE ROUGH FIELD

*Old moulds are broken in the North:*
*In the dark streets, firing starts. . . .*

I had never known sorrow,
Now it is a field I have inherited, and I till it.
— *from the Afghan*

The Greeks say it was the Turks who burned
down Smyrna. The Turks say it was the Greeks.
Who will discover the truth?
The wrong has been committed.
The important thing is who will redeem it?
— *George Seferis*

# PREFACE

This poem begins in the early Sixties, when I went to Belfast to receive a small poetry prize, the first, I think, to exist in that part of the world. (Ironically, the Irish papers hailed it as 'Dublin Poet wins Belfast Prize', so little were they accustomed to a poet of my background.) To deepen the paradox, the award was presented in the Assembly Rooms of the Presbyterian Church in Belfast, a vast Victorian building in the heart of the city. And as 'Like Dolmens round my Childhood' was being read, I heard the rumble of drums, preparing for 'The Twelfth', the annual Orange festival.

Bumping down towards Tyrone a few days later by bus, I had a kind of vision, in the medieval sense, of my home area, the unhappiness of its historical destiny. And of all such remote areas where the presence of the past is compounded with a bleak economic future, whether in Ulster, Brittany or the Highlands of Scotland. I managed to draft the opening and the close, but soon realised that I did not have the technique for so varied a task. Although living in Berkeley introduced me to the debate on open-form from *Paterson,* through Olson, to Duncan, I was equally drawn by rooted poets like MacDiarmid in *A Drunk Man.* . . . At intervals during the decade I returned to it, when the signs seemed right. An extreme Protestant organisation put me on its mailing list, for instance, and the only antidote I could find against such hatred was to absorb it into 'The Bread God'. And ten years later I was given another small award from the North to complete the manuscript.

Although, as the Ulster crisis broke, I felt as if I had been stirring a witch's cauldron, I never thought of the poem as tethered to any particular set of events. One explores an inheritance to free oneself and others, and if I sometimes saw the poem as taking over where the last bard of the O'Neills left off, the New Road I describe runs through Normandy as well as Tyrone. And experience of agitations in Paris and Berkeley taught me that the violence of disputing factions is more than a local phenomenon. But one must start from home — so the poem begins where I began myself, with a Catholic family in the townland of Garvaghey*, in the county of Tyrone, in the province of Ulster.

*Garvaghey: *Garbh acaidh*, a rough field

5

# I

# HOME AGAIN

*Lost in our separate work*
*We meet at dusk in a narrow lane.*
*I press back against a tree*
*To let him pass, but he brakes*
*Against our double loneliness*
*With: 'So you're home again!'*

# 1

*Vast changes have taken place, and
rulers have passed away, dynasties
fallen, since that glorious autumn
day when Lord Mountjoy, accom-
panied by his land steward, arrived
by coach in Omagh. . . .*

*Catching a bus at Victoria Station,*
Symbol of Belfast in its iron bleakness,
We ride through narrow huckster streets
(Small lamps bright before the Sacred Heart,
Bunting tagged for some religious feast)
To where Cavehill and Divis, stern presences,
Brood over a wilderness of cinemas and shops,
Victorian red-brick villas, framed with aerials,
Bushmill hoardings, Orange and Legion Halls.
A fringe of trees affords some ease at last
From all this dour, despoiled inheritance,
The shabby throughotherness of outskirts:
'God is Love', chalked on a grimy wall
Mocks a culture where constraint is all.

*His Lordship stood high with the
government of the day. He was
wealthy and had acquired, through
Charles Blount, the first Earl, an
immense tract of the O'Neill coun-
try. As he rode along no menacing
banner of that ancient sept frowned
down on him from* dún *or tower.*

Through half of Ulster that Royal Road ran
Through Lisburn, Lurgan, Portadown,
Solid British towns, lacking local grace.
Headscarved housewives in bulky floral skirts
Hugged market baskets on the plastic seats
Although it was near the borders of Tyrone —
End of the Pale, beginning of O'Neill —
Before a stranger turned a friendly face,
Yarning politics in Ulster monotone.
Bathos as we bumped all that twilight road,

Tales of the Ancient Order, Ulster's Volunteers:
Narrow fields wrought such division,
And narrow they were, though as darkness fell
Ruled by the evening star, which saw me home

*Hugh O'Neill was soundly*
*asleep by the banks of the*
*Tiber, where no bugle blast of*
*his fiery clansmen could ever*
*reach or rouse him. McArt's*
*stronghold was a mere tradi-*
*tion by the banks of the Strule.*
*His Lordship could ride easily*
*for the echoes of 'Lamh Dearg*
*Abus' had long since faded away*
*among the hills of the north. ...*
*'Broken was Tirowen's pride,*
*And vanquished Clanaboy.'*
— Ulster Herald

To a gaunt farmhouse on this busy road,
Bisecting slopes of plaintive moorland,
Where I assume old ways of walk and work
So easily, yet feel the sadness of return
To what seems still, though changing.
No Wordsworthian dream enchants me here
With glint of glacial corrie, totemic mountain,
But merging low hills and gravel streams,
Oozy blackness of bog-banks, tough upland grass;
Rough Field in the Gaelic and rightly named
As setting for a mode of life that passes on:
Harsh landscape that haunts me,
Well and stone, in the bleak moors of dream,
With all my circling a failure to return.

## 2

Hearing the cock crow in the dark,
The first thing to move in the desolate farmyard,
I lay awake to listen, the tripled shrill calls
As jagged and chill as water
While a pale movement of dawn
Began to climb and outline
The dark window-frame.

Those were my first mornings,
Fresh as Eden, with dew on the face,
Like first kiss, the damp air:
On dismantled flagstones,
From ash-smoored embers
Hands now strive to rekindle
That once leaping fire.

# 3

*On the recommendation of the Earl
of Belmore, H.M.L., the Lord
Chancellor has appointed the following
gentlemen to the Commission of
the Peace for Tyrone County; on behalf
and under the Seal of H.M. Queen
Victoria: Dr. J. J. Todd, Omagh; William
Anderson, The Grange, Tullyhogue;
Neil Bradley, Strabane; Robert Hall
Anderson, Sixmilecross; John Montague,
Garvaghey.*

Between small, whin-tough hills,
The first slated house in the district;
Garvaghey, with its ring of firs.
From a silvered daguerreotype
My grandfather, country lawyer,
Hedge schoolmaster, Redmondite,
Stares out, white beard curled
Like a seahorse. Hovering anonymous
In the background, his patient
Tight-corsetted wife prepares
Another meal to absorb the spirit
That stokes a patriarch's wit.
The children are kept out of sight,
All eight surviving; she'll die
With the eleventh.
                        Such posed
Conceit recalls post-Famine years
When Catholics regain the precious
Right to rise above their neighbours.
Labourers stooped in his fields while
John Montague presided at Petty Sessions

Or attended meetings of a Belfast firm.
Sundays, rattling the leather reins,
He drove a side-car over the Fox's Leap
To the dark glens of Altamuskin
Where the Tagues came from. A blend
Of wild Irish and Ulster Puritan —
The dram of poteen beside Cardinal Wiseman
In his bedroom — combine to make
A rustic gentleman.
                              Sixty years
Later, his succession was broken,
Sons scattered to Australia, Brooklyn.
The rotting side-car propped a hole
In the hedge, box lanterns askew.
All the sadness of a house in decay
Showed in the weed-grown cobbles,
The gaping stables. But the stacks
Still rode the stone-circled haggard
And the tall shed was walled high
And dry with turf, for the war years.
Then the wide tent of a hearth
Where Dagda's cauldron swung
Shrank to a coal-fired stove
And tiled stone.


# 4


THE COUNTRY FIDDLER

My uncle played the fiddle — more elegantly the violin —
A favourite at barn and crossroads dance,
He knew 'The Morning Star' and 'O'Neill's Lament'.

Bachelor head of a house full of sisters,
Runner of poor racehorses, spendthrift,
He left for the New World in an old disgrace.

He left his fiddle in the rafters
When he sailed, never played afterwards,
A rural art stilled in the discord of Brooklyn.

A heavily-built man, tranquil-eyed as an ox,
He ran a wild speakeasy, and died of it.
During the Depression many dossed in his cellar.

I attended his funeral in the Church of the Redemption,
Then, unexpected successor, reversed time
To return where he had been born.

During my schooldays the fiddle rusted
(The bridge fell away, the catgut snapped)
Reduced to a plaything, stinking of stale rosin.

The country people asked if I also had music
(All the family had had) but the fiddle was in pieces
And the rafters remade, before I discovered my craft.

Twenty years afterwards, I saw the church again,
And promised to remember my burly godfather
And his rural craft after this fashion:

So succession passes, through strangest hands.

# 5

LIKE DOLMENS ROUND MY CHILDHOOD . . .

Like dolmens round my childhood, the old people.

Jamie MacCrystal sang to himself,
A broken song without tune, without words;
He tipped me a penny every pension day,
Fed kindly crusts to winter birds.
When he died, his cottage was robbed,
Mattress and money-box torn and searched.
Only the corpse they didn't disturb.

Maggie Owens was surrounded by animals,
A mongrel bitch and shivering pups,
Even in her bedroom a she-goat cried.
She was a well of gossip defiled,
Fanged chronicler of a whole countryside;
Reputed a witch, all I could find
Was her lonely need to deride.

The Nialls lived along a mountain lane
Where heather bells bloomed, clumps of foxglove.
All were blind, with Blind Pension and Wireless.
Dead eyes serpent-flickered as one entered
To shelter from a downpour of mountain rain.
Crickets chirped under the rocking hearthstone
Until the muddy sun shone out again.

Mary Moore lived in a crumbling gatehouse,
Famous as Pisa for its leaning gable.
Bag-apron and boots, she tramped the fields
Driving lean cattle from a miry stable.
A by-word for fierceness, she fell asleep
Over love stories, *Red Star* and *Red Circle,*
Dreamed of gypsy love-rites, by firelight sealed.

Wild Billy Eagleson married a Catholic servant girl
When all his Loyal family passed on:
We danced round him shouting 'To hell with King Billy',
And dodged from the arc of his flailing blackthorn.
Forsaken by both creeds, he showed little concern
Until the Orange drums banged past in the summer
And bowler and sash aggressively shone.

Curate and doctor trudged to attend them,
Through knee-deep snow, through summer heat,
From main road to lane to broken path,
Gulping the mountain air with painful breath.
Sometimes they were found by neighbours,
Silent keepers of a smokeless hearth,
Suddenly cast in the mould of death.

Ancient Ireland, indeed! I was reared by her bedside,
The rune and the chant, evil eye and averted head,
Fomorian fierceness of family and local feud.
Gaunt figures of fear and of friendliness,
For years they trespassed on my dreams,
Until once, in a standing circle of stones,
I felt their shadows pass

Into that dark permanence of ancient forms.

# II

# THE LEAPING FIRE

I. M. BRIGID MONTAGUE (1876-1966)

*Each morning, from the corner*
*of the hearth, I saw a miracle*
*as you sifted the smoored ashes*
*to blow*
　　　　*a fire's sleeping remains*
*back to life, holding the burning brands*
*of turf, between work-hardened hands.*
*I draw on that fire....*

# 1

THE LITTLE FLOWER'S DISCIPLE

Old lady, I now celebrate
to whom I owe so much;
bending over me in darkness
a scaly tenderness of touch

skin of bony arm & elbow
sandpapered with work:
because things be to be done
and simplicity did not shirk

the helpless, hopeless task
of maintaining a family farm,
which meant, by legal fiction,
maintaining a family name.

The thongless man's boots,
the shapeless bag-apron:
would your favourite saint
accept the harness of humiliation

you bore constantly until
the hiss of milk into the pail
became as lonely a prayer as
your vigil at the altar rail.

Roses showering from heaven
upon Her uncorrupted body
after death, celebrated
the Little Flower's sanctity

& through the latticed grill
of your patron's enclosed order
an old French nun once threw me
a tiny sack of lavender.

So from the pressed herbs
of your least memory, sweetness exudes:
that of the meek and the selfless,
who should be comforted.

# 2

Nightly she climbs the
narrow length of the stairs
to kneel in her cold room
as if she would storm
heaven with her prayers

which, if they have power,
now reach across the quiet
night of death to where
instead of a worn rosary,
I tell these metal keys.

The pain of a whole family
she gathers into her hands:
the spent mother who died
to give birth to children
scattered to the four winds

who now creakingly arouse
from darkness, distance
to populate the corners
of this silent house
they once knew so well.

A draught-whipped candle
magnifies her shadow —
a frail body grown monstrous,
sighing in a trance
before the gilt crucifix —

& as the light gutters
the shadows gather to dance
on the wall of the next room
where, a schoolboy searching sleep,
I begin to touch myself.

The sap of another generation
fingering through a broken tree
to push fresh branches
towards a further light,
a different identity.

# 3

Your white hair
on the thin rack
of your shoulders

it is hard to
look into the eyes
of the dying

who carry away
a part of oneself —
a shared world

& you, whose life
was selflessness,
now die slowly

broken down by
process to a pale
exhausted beauty

the moon in her
last phase, caring
only for herself.

I lean over the
bed but you barely
recognize me &

when an image
forces entry —
'Is that John?

Bring me home,'
you whimper &
I see a house

shaken by traffic
until a fault runs
from roof to base

but your face has
already retired into
the blind, animal

misery of age
paying out your
rosary beads

hands twitching
as you drift
towards nothingness

# 4

A HOLLOW NOTE

Family legend held
that this frail
woman had heard
the banshee's wail

& on the night
she lay dying
I heard a low,
constant crying

over the indifferent
roofs of Paris —
the marsh bittern
or white owl sailing

from its foul
nest of bones
to warn me with
a hollow note

& among autobuses
& taxis, the shrill
paraphernalia of a
swollen city

I crossed myself
from rusty habit
before I realised
why I had done it.

# III

# THE BREAD GOD

FOR THOMAS MONTAGUE, SJ, ON HIS EIGHTIETH BIRTHDAY

*I break again into the lean parish of my art*
*Where huddled candles flare before a shrine*
*And men with caps in hand kneel stiffly down*
*To see the many-fanged monstrance shine.*

The Prime Minister, 10 Downing Street, London,  May 1, 1967

Dear Sir:

We take the liberty of writing to you on the serious subject of the proposed entry of Great Britain into Europe. After lengthy and serious discussions we have resolved to bring to your attention some constitutional issues which *must* be settled before the Government or the Sovereign can hand over their powers to an Assembly of Europe.

(1) The Commonwealth countries would still have a head of state, who would be subordinate to such Assembly should Her Majesty sign 'The Treaty of Rome'. . . .

(2) We fail to see how Her Majesty could be advised to sign away Her powers to an assembly, the membership of which is composed of people not of the Reformed Faith. What happens to the Coronation Oath?

. . . until a mandate is sought on these issues, we intend to take all possible constitutional action to prevent the Government from signing 'The Treaty of Rome'. We are currently studying the legal avenues with the view of obtaining an injunction against the British Government to prevent it from taking the United Kingdom into the European Common Market.

*The Belfast County Grand Lodge*
*Independent Loyal Orange Institution of Ireland*

*He who stood at midnight upon a little mount which rose behind
the chapel might see between five and six thousand torches, all
blazing together, and forming a level mass of red dusky light,
burning against the dark horizon. These torches were so close to
each other that their light seemed to blend, as if they had consti-
tuted one wide surface of flame; and nothing could be more pre-
ternatural-looking than the striking and devotional countenance
of those who were assembled at their midnight worship, when ob-
served beneath this canopy of fire. . . .*

CHRISTMAS MORNING

Lights outline a hill
As silently the people,
Like shepherd and angel
On that first morning,
March from Altcloghfin,
Beltany, Rarogan,
Under rimed hawthorn,
Gothic evergreen,
Grouped in the warmth
& cloud of their breath,
Along cattle paths
Crusted with ice,
Tarred roads to this
Grey country chapel
Where a gas-lamp hisses
To light the crib
Under the cross-beam's
Damp flaked message:
GLORIA IN EXCELSIS.

*Yes. I remember Carleton's description of Christmas in Tyrone, but things
had changed at the end of the century. Religion was at a pretty low ebb in
those days. We had one Mass at 10 o'clock on Sundays at which a handful
went to Communion. We went to Confession and Communion about every
four months. The priests did not take much interest in the people and did not
visit them except for sick calls. I think I became a priest because we were the
most respectable family in the parish and it was expected of me, but what I
really wanted to do was to join the army, which was out of the question. So
you see how your uncle became a Jesuit!*

Christmas, Melbourne, 1960

23

LATE-COMER

Hesitant step of a late-comer.
Fingers dip at the font, fly
Up to the roof of the forehead
With a sigh.
                    On St Joseph's
Outstretched arm, he hangs his cap,
Then spends a very pleasant mass
Studying the wen-marked heads
Of his neighbours, or gouging
His name in the soft wood
Of the choirloft, with the cross
Of his rosary beads.


In a plain envelope marked: IMPORTANT
THE BREAD GOD
*the* DEVIL *has* CHRIST *where he wants* HIM
A HELPLESS INFANT IN ARMS: A DEAD CHRIST ON THE CROSS
ROME'S CENTRAL ACT OF WORSHIP IS THE EUCHARISTIC WAFER!
IDOLATRY: THE WORST IDOL UNDER HEAVEN
NOSELESS, EYELESS, EARLESS, HELPLESS, SPEECHLESS.


CROWD

The crowds for Communion, heavy coat and black shawl,
Surge in thick waves, cattle thronged in a fair,
To the oblong of altar rails, and there
Where red-berried holly shines against gold
In the door of the tabernacle, wait patient
And prayerful and crowded, for each moment
Of silence, eyes closed, mouth raised
For the advent of the flesh-graced Word.

DEAR BROTHER!
ECUMENISM *is* THE NEW NAME *of the* WHORE OF BABYLON
SHE *who* SHITS *on the* SEVEN HILLS
ONE CHURCH, ONE STATE
WITH THE POPE THE HEAD OF THE STATE: BY RE-UNION
ROME MEANS ABSORPTION
UNIFORMITY MEANS TYRANNY
APISTS = PAPISTS
*But* GOD DELIGHTS IN VARIETY
NO *two leaves are* EXACTLY *alike!*


AFTER MASS

      Coming out of the chapel
      The men were already assembled
      Around the oak-tree,
      Solid brogues, thick coats,
      Staring at the women,
      Sheltering cigarettes.

      Once a politician came
      Climbed on the graveyard wall
      And they listened to all
      His plans with the same docility;
      Eyes quiet, under caps
      Like sloped eaves.

      Nailed to the wet bark
      The notice of a football match;
      Pearses *vs* Hibernians
      Or a Monster Carnival
      In aid of Church Funds
      Featuring Farrell's Band.

LOYALISTS REMEMBER!
MILLIONS *have been* MURDERED *for refusing to* GROVEL
*Before Rome's Mass-Idol :* THE HOST!
*King Charles* I *and his Frog Queen Henrietta* GLOAT *in their letters*
*that they have almost* EXTERMINATED THE PROTESTANTS OF IRELAND
*The* PRIESTS *in every* PARISH *were told to record* HOW MANY KILLED!
*Under* ROGER MOORE *and* SIR PHELIM O'NEIL
*Instruments of* ROME
*40,000 loyal Protestants were* MASSACRED *like game-fowl*
IN ONE NIGHT
*Cromwell went to Ireland*
TO STOP
*The Catholics murdering Protestants!*

PENAL ROCK: ALTAMUSKIN

To learn the massrock's lesson, leave your car,
Descend frost-gripped steps to where
A humid moss overlaps the valley floor.
Crisp as a pistol-shot, the winter air
Recalls poor Tagues, folding the nap of their frieze
Under one knee, long suffering as beasts,
But parched for that surviving sign of grace,
The bog-latin murmur of their priest.
A crude stone oratory, carved by a cousin,
Commemorates the place. For two hundred years
People of our name have sheltered in this glen
But now all have left. A few flowers
Wither on the altar, so I melt a ball of snow
From the hedge into their rusty tin before I go.

*I sometimes wonder if anyone could have brought the two sides to-*
*gether. Your father, I know, was very bitter about having to leave*
*but when I visited home before leaving for the Australian mission, I*
*found our Protestant neighbours friendly, and yet we had lost any*
*position we had in the neighbourhood. You realise, of course, that*
*all this has nothing to do with religion; perhaps this new man will*
*find a way to resolve the old hatreds....*

26

I saw the Pope breaking stones on Friday,
A blind parson sewing a patchwork quilt,
Two bishops cutting rushes with their croziers,
Roaring Meg firing rosary beads for cannonballs,
Corks in boats afloat on the summit of the Sperrins,
A severed head speaking with a grafted tongue,
A snail paring Royal Avenue with a hatchet,
British troops firing on the Shankill,
A mill and a forge on the back of a cuckoo,
The fox sitting conceitedly at a window chewing tobacco,
And a curlew in flight
                              surveying
                                   a United Ireland....

# IV

# A SEVERED HEAD

*Sir Thomas Phillips made a journey from Coleraine to Dungannon, through the wooded country . . . and thereupon wrote to Salisbury, expressing . . . his unfeigned astonishment at the sight of so many cattle and such abundance of grain. . . . The hillsides were literally covered with cattle . . . the valleys were clothed in the rich garniture of ripening barley and oats; while the woods swarmed with swine . . . 20,000 of these being easily fattened yearly in the forest of Glenconkeyne alone.*
— George Hill: *An Historical Account of the Plantation in Ulster*


*Our geographers do not forget what entertainment the Irish of Tyrone gave to a mapmaker about the end of the late great rebellion; for, one Barkeley being appointed by the late Earl of Devonshire to draw a true and perfect map of the north parts of Ulster . . . when he came into Tyrone the inhabitants took off his head. . . .* — Sir John Davies


*And who ever heard*
*Such a sight unsung*
*As a severed head*
*With a grafted tongue?*
— Traditional

# 1

May, and the air is light
On eye, on hand. As I take
The mountain road, my former step
Doubles mine, driving cattle
To the upland fields. Between
Shelving ditches of whitethorn
They sway their burdensome
Bodies, tempted at each turn
By hollows of sweet grass,
Pale clover, while memory,
A restive sally-switch, flicks
Across their backs.
                    The well
Is still there, a half-way mark
Between two cottages, opposite
The gate into Danaghy's field,
But above the protective dry-
Stone rim, the plaiting thorns
Have not been bill-hooked back
And a thick *glaur* floats.
No need to rush to head off
The cattle from sinking soft
Muzzles into leaf-smelling
Spring water.
                    From the farm
Nearby, I hear a yard tap gush
And a collie bark, to check
My presence. Our farmhands
Lived there, wife and children
In twin white-washed cells,
An iron roof burning in summer.
Now there is a kitchen extension
With radio aerial, rough outhouses
For coal and tractor. A housewife
Smiles good-day as I step through
The fluff and dust of her walled
Farmyard, solicited by raw-necked
Stalking turkeys

                    to where cart
Ruts shape the ridge of a valley,
One of many among the switch-
Back hills of what old chroniclers
Called the Star Bog. Croziered
Fern, white scut of *ceannbhán*,
Spars of bleached bog fir jutting
From heather, make a landscape
So light in wash it must be learnt
Day by day, in shifting detail,
Out to the blue Sperrins.
'I like to look across,' said
Barney Horisk leaning on his *sleán*
'And think of all the people
Who have bin.'
                    Like shards
Of a lost culture, the slopes
Are strewn with cabins, deserted
In my lifetime. Here the older
People sheltered, the Blind Nialls,
Big Ellen, who had been a Fair-
Day prostitute. The bushes cramp
To the evening wind as I reach
The road's end. Jamie MacCrystal
Lived in the final cottage,
A trim grove of mountain ash
Soughing protection round his walls
And bright painted gate. The thatch
Has slumped in, white dust of nettles
On the flags. Only the shed remains
In use for calves, although fuschia
Bleeds by the wall, and someone has
Propped a yellow cartwheel
Against the door.

## 2

All around, shards of a lost tradition:
From the Rough Field I went to school
In the Glen of the Hazels. Close by
Was the bishopric of the Golden Stone;
The cairn of Carleton's homesick poem.

Scattered over the hills, tribal-
And placenames, uncultivated pearls.
No rock or ruin, *dún* or dolmen
But showed memory defying cruelty
Through an image-encrusted name.

The heathery gap where the Rapparee,
Shane Barnagh, saw his brother die —
On a summer's day the dying sun
Stained its colours to crimson:
So breaks the heart, Brish-mo-Cree.

The whole landscape a manuscript
We had lost the skill to read,
A part of our past disinherited;
But fumbled, like a blind man,
Along the fingertips of instinct.

The last Gaelic speaker in the parish
When I stammered my school Irish
One Sunday after mass, crinkled
A rusty litany of praise:
*Tá an Ghaeilge againn arís* . . . *

*Tír Eoghain:* Land of Owen,
Province of the O'Niall;
The ghostly tread of O'Hagan's
Barefoot gallowglasses marching
To merge forces in Dún Geanainn

Push southward to Kinsale!
Loudly the war-cry is swallowed
In swirls of black rain and fog
As Ulster's pride, Elizabeth's foemen,
Founder in a Munster bog.

* 'We have the Irish again.'

'O'Neill: A name more in price
than to be called Caesar.'
— Sir George Carew


# 3

CON BACACH, 1542

Heralded by trumpeters,
Prefaced by a bishop,
Sided by earls, Con
The Lame limps down
The palace at Greenwich.
Twenty angels for
A fur-lined gown,
Ten white pounds
To the College of Arms
For a new escutcheon
That he may kneel on
The deep strewn rushes
To hear Henry's command;
When the bugles sound —
Forty shillings, by custom,
Must go to the captain —
His knee lifts rustily
From English ground:
*Arise, Earl of Tyrone.*

SEÁN AN DIOMAS, 1562

Swarthy and savage as
The dream of a conquistador,
Seán O'Niall, Shane
The Proud struts before
The first Elizabeth.
Her fine-hosed courtiers
Stare at his escort
Of tall gallowglasses,
Long hair curling
Over saffron shirts
With, on each shoulder —
Under the tangle of
The forbidden glib —
The dark death-sheen
Of the battle axe.

## HUGH, 1599

Around the table
Of the Great O'Neill
(Crushed bracken or
A stone slab, under
A cloudless heaven)
Sir John Harington sees
The princely children
In velvet jerkin
And gold lace, after
The English fashion
With a bodyguard of
Beardless, half-naked
Boys, all listening
Meek as spaniels
While, with the aid
Of the shy poet tutor
He reads his translation
Of Ariosto's canto
On Fortune's Wheel
Whither 'runs a
Restless round'.

## AFTER KINSALE, 1604

A messenger from the Pale
Found the hunted rebel
Living, like a woodkerne,
In the wet meadows near
His broken coronation stone.
From Tullyhogue
He rides to Mellifont
To kneel for an hour
Before the Lord Deputy
'Most sorrowfully imploring'
Her Sacred Majesty,
Promising to abjure
'All barbarous custom'
His tribal title, O Niall.
Mountjoy embraces him
Omitting to mention
That the red-haired queen
He so reverently entreats
Is dead a week.

# 4

THE FLIGHT OF THE EARLS

*This was a distinguished crew for one ship; for it is indeed
certain that the sea had not supported, and the winds had not
wafted from Ireland, in modern times, a party of one ship who
would have been more illustrious, or noble in point of genealogy,
or more renowned for deeds, valour or high achievements. . . .*
— Annals of the Four Masters

>The fiddler settles in
>to his playing so easily;
>rosewood box tucked under chin,
>saw of rosined bow
>& angle of elbow
>
>that the mind elides
>for a while what he plays:
>hornpipe or reel to warm
>us up well, heel or toecap
>twitching in tune
>
>till the sound expands
>in the slow climb of a lament.
>As by some forest campfire
>listeners draw near, to honour
>a communal loss
>
>& a shattered procession
>of anonymous suffering
>files through the brain:
>burnt houses, pillaged farms,
>a province in flames.

*We have killed, burnt and despoiled all along the Lough to
within four miles of Dungannon . . . in which journeys we
have killed above a hundred of all sorts, besides such as we
have burned, how many I know not. We spare none, of what
quality or sex soever, and it had bred much terror in the
people who heard not a drum nor saw not a fire of long time.*
— Chichester to Mountjoy, Spring 1607

With an intricate
& mournful mastery
the thin bow glides & slides,
assuaging like a bardic poem,
our tribal pain —

Disappearance & death
of a world, as down Lough Swilly
the great ship, encumbered with nobles,
swells its sails for Europe:
The Flight of the Earls.

# 5

A GRAFTED TONGUE

(Dumb,
bloodied, the severed
head now chokes to
speak another tongue —

As in
a long suppressed dream,
some stuttering garb-
led ordeal of my own)

An Irish
child weeps at school
repeating its English.
After each mistake

The master
gouges another mark
on the tally stick
hung about its neck

Like a bell
on a cow, a hobble
on a straying goat.
To slur and stumble

In shame
the altered syllables
of your own name;
to stray sadly home

And find
the turf-cured width
of your parent's hearth
growing slowly alien:

In cabin
and field, they still
speak the old tongue.
You may greet no one.

To grow
a second tongue, as
harsh a humiliation
as twice to be born.

Decades later
that child's grandchild's
speech stumbles over lost
syllables of an old order.

# 6

Yet even English in these airts
Took a lawless turn, as who
Would not stroll by Bloody Brae
To Black Lough, or guddle trout
In a stream called the Routing Burn?

Or rest a while on Crooked Bridge
Up the path to Crow Hill;
Straight by Ania's Cove to Spur Royal,
Then round by Duck Island
To Greenmount and Newtownsaville?

A last look over the dark ravine
Where that red-tufted rebel,
The Todd, out-leaped the pack;
Turning home by Favour Royal
And the forests of Dourless Black.

And what of stone-age Seskilgreen,
Tullycorker and Tullyglush?
Names twining braid Scots and Irish,
Like Fall Brae, springing native
As a whitethorn bush?

A high, stony place — bogstreams,
Not milk and honey — but our own:
From the Glen of the Hazels
To the Golden Stone may be
The longest journey
                    I have ever gone.

# V

# THE FAULT

*I hope Lynch will not be executed for I know he knew nothing of this till the last moment, though at the last meeting of the Council he consented by his silence when I alone opposed it. I was told Tyrone was not Ireland, and that I could not take a correct view of the situation from the position of Tyrone.*
— Dr Patrick McCartan, May 1916

*Then came the Great War. . . . Great empires have been overturned. . . . The position of countries has been violently altered. The modes of thought of men, the whole outlook on affairs, the grouping of parties, all have encountered tremendous changes. . . . But as the deluge subsides and the waters fall short we see the dreary steeples of Fermanagh and Tyrone emerging once again. The integrity of their quarrel is one of the few institutions that has been unaltered by the cataclysm.*
— Winston Churchill, 1922

# 1

STELE FOR A NORTHERN REPUBLICAN

Once again, with creased forehead
and trembling hands, my father calls
me from stifling darkness. . . .
Little enough I know of your struggle,
although you come to me more and more,
free of that heavy body armour
you tried to dissolve with alcohol,
a pale face straining in dream light
like a fish's belly
                          upward to life.
Hesitantly, I trace your part in
the holy war to restore our country,
slipping from home to smoke
an absentee's mansion, concoct
ambushes. Games turned serious
when the cross-fire at Falban
riddled the tender of policemen,
one bleeding badly
                          stretched upon
the stone flags of our kitchen,
your sisters moving in a whisper
of blood and bandages. Strange war
when the patrol scouted bales
of fodder, stray timber, tar
to prepare those sheltering walls
for reprisal's savage flames
if he should die!
                          That night
you booked into a Strabane hotel.
'Locals were rarely used for jobs:
orders of the Dublin organizer,
shot afterwards, by his own side.'
A generation later, the only sign
of your parochial struggle was
when the plough rooted rusty guns,
dull bayonets, in some rushy glen
for us to play with.

                    Although again
and again, the dregs of disillusion
churned in our Northern parents' guts
to set their children's teeth on edge;
my mother hobbling to the shed
to burn the Free State uniforms
her two brothers had thrown off
(frugal, she saved the buttons):
my father, home from the boat at Cobh,
staring in anger at a Redmond
Commemoration stamp
                            or tearing to
flitters the polite Masscard sent
by a Catholic policeman. But what if
you have no country to set before Christ,
only a broken province? No parades,
fierce medals, will mark Tyrone's re-birth,
betrayed by both South and North;
so lie still, difficult old man,
you were right to choose a Brooklyn slum
rather than a half-life in this
by-passed and dying place.

## 2

THE SAME FAULT

When I am angry, sick or tired
A line on my forehead pulses,
The line on my left temple
Opened by an old car accident.
My father had the same scar
In the same place, as if
The same fault ran through
Us both: anger, impatience,
A stress born of violence.

## 3

SOUND OF A WOUND

Who knows
the sound a wound makes?
    Scar tissue
can rend, the old hurt
    tear open as
the torso of the fiddle
    groans to
carry the tune, to carry
    the pain of
a lost (slow herds of cattle
    roving over
soft meadow, dark bogland)
    pastoral rhythm.

    I assert
a civilisation died here;
    it trembles
underfoot where I walk these
    small, sad hills:
it rears in my blood stream
    when I hear
a bleat of Saxon condescension,
    Westminster
to hell, it is less than these

strangely carved
five-thousand-year resisting stones,
    that lonely cross.

    This bitterness
I inherit from my father, the
    swarm of blood
to the brain, the vomit surge
    of race hatred,
the victim seeing the oppressor,
    bold Jacobean
planter, or gadget-laden marine,
    who has scattered
his household gods, used
    his people
as servants, flushed his women
    like game.


# 4

THE CAGE

My father, the least happy
man I have known. His face
retained the pallor
of those who work underground:
the lost years in Brooklyn
listening to a subway
shudder the earth.

But a traditional Irishman
who (released from his grille
in the Clark Street I.R.T.)
drank neat whiskey until
he reached the only element
he felt at home in
any longer: brute oblivion.

And yet picked himself
up, most mornings,
to march down the street
extending his smile

to all sides of the good,
(all-white) neighbourhood
belled by St Teresa's church.

When he came back
we walked together
across fields of Garvaghey
to see hawthorn on the summer
hedges, as though
he had never left;
a bend of the road

which still sheltered
primroses. But we
did not smile in
the shared complicity
of a dream, for when
weary Odysseus returns
Telemachus should leave.

Often as I descend
into subway or underground
I see his bald head behind
the bars of the small booth;
the mark of an old car
accident beating on his
ghostly forehead.

# VI

# A GOOD NIGHT

# 1

THE LAST SHEAF

We meet that evening in The Last Sheaf
Which has gained mocking notoriety
Since the boss began to diminish
His own stock. A distempered house
At a crossroads, we mount guard
On neighbours cycling heavily past
As we jostle at the deal bar
In a brackish stour of stout,
Paraffin, stale bread.
                              After hours
All hands shift to the kitchen,
Snap down the blinds! Our light
Is a grease-fattened candle, but
In our gloomy midnight cave
No one minds, we have reached
The singing stage. 'The Orange Flute',
'The Mountains of Pomeroy', the songs
That survive in this sparse soil
Are quavered out, until someone
Remembers to call on Packy Farrell
'To say a song'.
                         With the almost
Professional shyness of the folk-singer
He keeps us waiting, until he rises,
Head forced back, eyeballs blind.
'An Bunnán Buí'. As the Gaelic

46

Rises and recedes, swirling deep
To fall back, all are silent,
Tentacles of race seeking to sound
That rough sadness. At the climax
He grips the chair before him
Until the knuckles whiten —
Sits down abruptly as he rose.
Man looks at man, the current
Of community revived to a near-
Ly perfect round. . . .

                      Soon broken
As talk expands, in drunken detail.
'I said to him': 'He swore to me.'
With smart-alec roughness, Henry
Rakes up our family history:
'Was it patriotism, or bankruptcy?'
Austin Donnelly remembers our fight
Over a swallow's nest, a caning
For peering under the Girls' Lavatory.
An owl-sad child, shaken from sleep,
Watches us, in a tatty nightshirt.
'A crying shame,' sighs one, but his
Publican father is so far gone, he
No longer bothers to trek to the bar
But strikes bottles on the flange
Of the Rayburn, until the floor
Is littered with green splinters
Of glass, tintops.

                      It is the usual
Grotesque, half-animal evening so
Common in Ireland, with much glum
Contrariness, much disappearing
Into the darkness, before we group
Outside, trying to mutter 'Goodnight'.
My companions now feel the need
To continue. Fit as fiddles,
Fresh as daisies, we plan the next move;
The moon on the road is a river
Of light, leading to new adventure. . . .

## 2

TACTILE

THE FIGHT

When I found the swallow's
Nest under the bridge —
Ankle-deep in the bog stream,
Traffic drumming overhead —
I was so pleased, I ran
To fetch a school companion
To share the nude fragility
Of the shells, lightly freckled
With colour, in their cradle
Of feathers, twigs, earth.

It was still breast warm
Where I curved in my hand
To count them, one by one
Into his cold palm, a kind
Of trophy or offering. Turn-
Ing my back, to scoop out
The last, I heard him run
Down the echoing hollow
Of the bridge. Splashing
After, I bent tangled in
Bull wire at the bridge's
Mouth, when I saw him take
And break them, one by one
Against a sunlit stone.

For minutes we fought
Standing and falling in
The river's brown spate,
And I would still fight
Though now I can forgive.

To worship or destroy beauty —
That double edge of impulse
I recognise, by which we live;
But also the bitter paradox
Of betraying love to harm,
Then lungeing, too late,
With fists, to its defence.

# 3

Three things to startle that day:
The flat, helpless way Henry's milk
Horse fell, as we raced to school,
And how, as we tiptoed in late,
The damp coats of the scholars
Stood breathing in the hall.
Last, at lunchtime, as the boys
Scuffled a string and paper ball
Over the gravel, a white Catalina
From the Erne base (an old pupil)
Rose out of a hole in the hedge,
Sudden as a flying swan, to circle
Over the school in salutation
And fold into cloud again.

# 4

Plan the next move. 'Whereabouts?
Don't forget the case of stout.'
Which only means that, dragging
A crate of bottles between us,
A rump parliament of old friends
Spend the lees of the night in
A mountain cottage, swapping
Stories, till cock-crow warns,
Then stagger home, drunk as coots,
Through the sleeping countryside.

A gate clangs, I grope against
A tent-fold of darkness until
Eye accepts the animal shape
Of the hedge, the sphere of
Speckled sky, the pale, damp
Fields breathing on either side.
The lane is smoothly tarred
Downhill to the humped bridge
Where I peer uncertainly over,
Lured towards sense by the
Unseen rattle of this mountain
Stream, whose lowland idlings
Define my townland's shape.

I climbed to its source once,
A journey perilous, through
The lifeless, lichened thorn
Of MacCrystal's Glen, a thread
Of water still leading me on
Past stale bog-cuttings, grey
Shapes slumped in rusty bracken,
Littered with fir's white bone:
Stranded mammoths! The water's
Thin music unwinding upwards
Till, high on a ledge of reeds
And heather, I came upon
A pool of ebony water
Fenced by rocks . . .

                    Legend
Declared a monster trout
Lived there, so I slipped
A hand under the fringe of
Each slick rock, splitting
The skin of turning froth
To find nothing but that
Wavering pulse leading to
The central heart where
The spring beat, so icy-cold
I shiver now in recollection,
Hearing its brisk, tireless
Movement over the pebbles
Beneath my feet . . .
                    Was that
The ancient trout of wisdom
I meant to catch? As I plod
Through the paling darkness
Details emerge, and memory
Warms. Old Danaghy raging
With his stick, to keep our
Cows from a well, that now
Is boarded up, like himself.
Here his son and I robbed a
Bee's nest, kicking the combs
Free; our boots smelt sweetly
For days afterwards. Snowdrop
In March, primrose in April,
Whitethorn in May, cardinal's
Fingers of foxglove dangling
All summer: every crevice held
A secret sweetness. Remembering,
I seem to smell wild honey
On my face.
                    And plunge
Down the hillside, singing
In a mood of fierce elation.
My seven league boots devour
Time and space as I crash
Through the last pools of
Darkness. All around, my
Neighbours sleep, but I am
In possession of their past

(The pattern history weaves
From one small backward place)
Marching through memory magnified:
Each grassblade bends with
Translucent beads of moisture
And the bird of total meaning
Stirs upon its hidden branch.

As I reach the last lap
The seventh sense of drunkenness —
That extra pilot in the head —
Tells me I am being watched
And, wheeling, I confront a clump
Of bullocks. Inert in grass,
They gaze at me, saucer-eyed,
Turning their slow surprise
Upon their tongue. *Store cattle:*
*The abattoirs of old England*
*Will soon put paid to them.* In
A far meadow, the corncrake
Turns its rusty ratchet and
I find myself rounding the
Last corner towards the black
Liquid gleam of the main road.

# 5

ROSELAND

And there, on a ravaged hillock
    overlooking the road,
the raw inheritor of this place,
    an unfinished hall.
Stung to soberness in the dawn
    I sway and stare.
Its blank eyes — gaps in concrete —
    stare blindly back.

*Seemsh no escape. Poet and object*
    *must conshumate.*
No lyric memory softens the fact —
    this stone idol

could house more hopes than any
    verse of mine.
I eye its girdered skeleton
    with brute respect.

Three miles away, a gutted castle
    stands; Sir John's
which my father helped to burn.
    Its elegant remains
still dominate the district, as
    now this Roseland
may, a concrete prow cargoed
    with vague dreams.

The shiny roofs of cars, shoals
    of minnows, may
swim around it, pairs stumble from
    the wide light
of the door to the narrow privacy
    of plastic seats.
A sigh, a kiss, hands wander
    near thin skirts

as music shakes & pounds.
    An industry built
on loneliness, setting the young
    to clamber over
each other, brief as mayflies
    in their hunger
for novelty, for flashing
    energy & change . . .

# VII

# HYMN TO THE NEW OMAGH ROAD

*As the bulldozer bites into the tree-ringed hillfort*
*Its grapnel jaws lift the mouse, the flower,*
*With equal attention, and the plaited twigs*
*And clay of the bird's nest, shaken by the traffic,*
*Fall from a crevice under the bridge*
*Into the slow-flowing mud-choked stream*
*Below the quarry, where the mountain trout*
*Turns up its pale belly to die.*

# 1

*Loss*

Item: The shearing away of an old barn
   criss-cross of beams where pigeons moan
   high small window where the swallow built
   white-washed dry-stone walls.

Item: The suppression of stone lined paths
   old potato-boiler full of crocuses
   overhanging lilac or laburnum
   sweet pea climbing the fence.

Item: The filling-in of chance streams
   uncovered wells, all unchannelled sources
   of water that might weaken foundations
   bubbling over the macadam.

Item: The disappearance of all signs
   of wild life, wren's or robin's nest,
   a rabbit nibbling a coltsfoot leaf,
   a stray squirrel or water rat.

Item: The uprooting of wayside hedges
   with their accomplices, devil's bit and pee the bed,
   prim rose and dog rose, an unlawful
   assembly of thistles.

Item: The removal of all hillocks
   and humps, superstition styled fairy forts
   and long barrows, now legally to be regarded
   as obstacles masking a driver's view.

*Gain*

Item: 10 men from the district being for a period of time fully
employed, their 10 wives could buy groceries and clothes to
send 30 children content to school for a few months, and
raise local merchants' hearts by paying their bills.

Item: A man driving from Belfast to Londonderry can arrive
a quarter of an hour earlier, a lorry load of goods ditto,
thus making Ulster more competitive in the international
market.

Item: A local travelling from the prefabricated suburbs of by-
passed villages can manage an average of 50 rather than
40 m.p.h. on his way to see relatives in Omagh hospital or
lunatic asylum.

Item: The dead of Garvaghey Graveyard (including my grand-
father) can have an unobstructed view — the trees having
been sheared away for a carpark — of the living passing at
great speed, sometimes quick enough to come straight in:

> *Let it be clear*
> *That I do not grudge my grandfather*
> *This long delayed pleasure!*
> *I like the idea of him*
> *Rising from the rotting boards of the coffin*
> *With his JP's white beard*
> *And penalising drivers*
> *For travelling faster*
> *Than jaunting cars*

# 2

From the quarry behind the school
the crustacean claws of the excavator
rummage to withdraw a payload,
a giant's bite. . . .

*'Tis pleasant for to take a stroll by Glencull Waterside*
*On a lovely evening in spring (in nature's early pride);*
*You pass by many a flowery bank and many a shady dell,*
*Like walking through enchanted land where fairies used to dwell*

        Tuberous tentacles
of oak, hawthorn, buried pignut,
the topsoil of a living shape
of earth lifts like a scalp
to lay open

*The trout are rising to the fly; the lambkins sport and play;*
*The pretty feathered warblers are singing by the way;*
*The black birds' and the thrushes' notes, by the echoes multiplied,*
*Do fill the vale with melody by Glencull Waterside.*

        slipping sand,
shale, compressed veins of rock,
old foundations, a soft chaos
to be swallowed wholesale,
masticated, regurgitated
by the mixer.

*Give not to me the rugged scenes of which some love to write —*
*The beetling cliffs, o'erhanging crags and the eagle in full flight,*
*But give to me the fertile fields (the farmer's joy and pride)*
*The homestead and the orchards fine by Glencull Waterside.*

        Secret places,
birds' nests, animal paths,
ghosts of children hunkering
down snail-glistering slopes
spin through iron cylinders to
resume new life as a pliant stream
of building material.

*These scenes bring recollections back to comrades scattered wide*
*Who used with me to walk these banks in youthful manly pride;*
*They've left their boyhood's happy homes and crossed o'er oceans wide*
*Now but in dreamland may they walk by Glencull Waterside.*

                    A brown stain
seeps away from where the machine
rocks and groans to itself, dis-
colouring the grass, thickening
the current of the trout stream
which flows between broken banks —
the Waterside a smear of mud —
towards the reinforced bridge
of the new road.

# VIII

# PATRIOTIC SUITE

FOR SEÁN Ó RIADA

# 1

## THE LURE

Again that note! A weaving
melancholy, like a bird crossing
moorland;
              ice film on a corrie
opening inward, soundless harp-
strings of rain:
              the pathos
of last letters in the 1916 Room,
'Mother, I thank . . .'
                    a podgy landmine,
Pearse's swordstick leading to a care-
fully profiled picture.
                    That point
where folk and art meet, murmurs
*Herr Doktor* as
              the wail of tin
whistle climbs against fiddle and
the *bodhrán* begins —
                    lost cry
of the yellow bittern!

# 2

The mythic lyre shrunk to country size:
The clatter of brogues on the flagstones,
The colourless dram of poteen —
Is that the world we were made for?

# 3

*Smell of appleblossom in the air,*
*Step of a huntress on the stair.*

In Bedford Park a young man waits
Still warm at the heart of family
But fearful what life, the hazard
Of his slight gift, holds in store:

'I was about to learn that the poet
Must be shaped by luckless luck
Into saint, lover or philosopher.'

*Smell of appleblossom in the air,*
*Step of a goddess on the stair.*


# 4

Symbolic depth-charge of music
Releases a national dream;
From clerk to paladin
In a single violent day.
Files of men from shattered buildings
(Slouch hat, blunt Mauser gun)
Frame the freedom that they won.

The bread queue, the messianic
Agitator of legend
Arriving on the train —
Christ and socialism —
Wheatfield and factory
Vivid in the sun:
Connolly's dream, if any one's.

All revolutions are interior
The displacement of spirit;
By the arrival of fact,
Ceaseless as cloud across sky,
Sudden as sun.
Tremor of a butterfly
Modifies everything.

# 5

The tribes merged into the hills,
The ultimate rocks where seals converse.
There they supped rain-water, ate sparse
Berries and (grouped around slow fires
At evening) comforted themselves
With runics of verse.

The nation forgot them until
There was a revolution. Then soldiers
Clambered the slopes, saluting
In friendliness: 'Come down!
You are the last pride of our race,
Herdsmen aristocrats, who have kept the faith.'

As they strayed through the vertical cities
Everyone admired their blue eyes, open smiles
(Vowels, like flowers, caught in the teeth)
The nervous majesty of their gait:
To the boredom of pavements they brought
The forgotten grace of the beast.

Soon townspeople tired of them,
Began to deride their smell, their speech.
Some returned. Others stayed behind,
Accommodating themselves to a new language.
In either case, they may be dying out.
A tragedy anticipated in the next Government Report.

# 6

THE ENTERPRISE

The train crawls across a bridge:
Through the cantilevered interstices —
A lace curtain monstrously magnified —
We overlook the sprawling town.

Row after row of council cottages
Ride the hill, curving up to the church
Or down to the docks
Where a crane tilts into emptiness.

Here nothing has been planned —
Assembled, yes, casual
And coarse as detritus,
Affronting eye and mind.

Only a drift of smoke
And the antlike activity of cars
Indicate life; with the wild flap
Of laundry in a thousand backyards.

Soon we are running through summer fields
Where a roller is at work
Bruising neat stripes of corn
Under hawthorn hedges, patterned in white flame.


# 7

COOLE PARK & ABBEY THEATRE 1951

The visitor to Coole Park
in search of a tradition
finds
          a tangled alley-way
a hint of foundation wall
(the kitchen floor)
                    high wire
to protect the famous beech-tree
from raw initials
                    and a lake
bereft of swans.


In this gutted building, a young man might stand,
Watching a fire hose play, like a soothing hand.
It has earned little of his heart, beyond the abstract
Duty and respect, accorded a public monument.

# 8

*During 1960/61 the Irish attained*
*many high positions abroad and*
*the national economy, for the first*
*time in history, showed an upward*
*trend. Only the Vatican continued*
*to ignore us.*

World-witnessed, our spiritual empire
After years so long enduring
That suffering became a form of speech
With all our songs plangent or soft:
Does fate at last relent
With a trade expansion of 5 per cent?

Now the unsmiling Saxon, surprised
And diffident, greets an equal
As, exemplary in the Congo,
Rational in the UN,
We prospect the lands beyond
Kipling's setting sun.

Already a shocked Belfast beholds
A black-veiled Queen enter the Vatican.
Through Washington and Canterbury
All roads lead to Rome.
Granted a saint, we might shepherd
Another Dark Ages home.

# 9

At the Fleadh Cheoil in Mullingar
There were two sounds, the breaking
Of glass, and the background pulse
Of music. Young girls roamed
The streets with eager faces,
Shoving for men.  Bottles in
Hand, they rowed out a song:
*Puritan Ireland's dead and gone,*
*A myth of O'Connor and Ó Faoláin.*

In the early morning the lovers
Lay on both sides of the canal
Listening on Sony transistors
To the agony of Pope John.
Yet it didn't seem strange or blasphemous,
This ground bass of death and
Resurrection, as we strolled along:
*Puritan Ireland's dead and gone,*
*A myth of O'Connor and Ó Faoláin.*

Further on, breasting the wind
Waves of the deserted grain harbour,
A silent pair, a cob and his pen,
Most nobly linked. Everything then
In our casual morning vision
Seemed to flow in one direction,
Lines simple as a song:
*Puritan Ireland's dead and gone,*
*A myth of O'Connor and Ó Faoláin.*

## 10

The gloomy images of a provincial catholicism

(in a thousand schoolrooms
children work quietly while
Christ bleeds on the wall)

wound in a native music
curlew echoing tin whistle
to eye-swimming melancholy

is that our offering?

While all Europe seeks
new versions of old ways,
the hammer of Boulez swing-
ing to Eastern harmonies.

From 1960 the Gross National Product . . .

Sight of the Skelligs at sunset
restores our Hy-Brasil:
the Atlantic expands on the cliffs
the herring gull claims the air

again that note!
                    above a self-drive car.

# IX

# A NEW SIEGE

FOR BERNADETTE DEVLIN

*Once again, it happens.*
*Under a barrage of stones*
*and flaring petrol bombs*
*the blunt, squat shape of*
*an armoured car glides*
*into the narrow streets*
*of the Catholic quarter*
*leading a file of helmet-*
*ed, shielded riot police;*
*once again, it happens,*
*like an old Troubles film,*
*run for the last time. . . .*

Lines of history
    lines of power
the long sweep
    of the Bogside
under the walls
    up to Creggan
the black muzzle
    of Roaring Meg
staring dead on
    cramped houses
the jackal shapes
    of James's army
watching the city
    stiffen in siege

SMALL SHOT HATH
    POURED LIKE HAIL
THE GREAT GUNS
    SHAKEN OUR WALLS
a spectral garrison
    no children left
sick from eating
    horseflesh, vermin
curs fattened on
    the slain Irish
still flaunting
    the bloody flag
of 'No Surrender'
    GOD HAS MADE US
AN IRON PILLAR
    AND BRAZEN WALLS
AGAINST THIS LAND.

Lines of defiance
    lines of discord
near the Diamond
    brisk with guns
British soldiers
    patrol the walls
the gates between
    Ulster Catholic
Ulster Protestant
    a Saracen slides
past the Guildhall
    a black Cuchulainn
bellowing against
    the Scarlet Whore
twin races petrified
    the volcanic ash
of religious hatred

Symbol of Ulster
    these sloping streets
blackened walls
    sick at heart and
seeking a sign
    the flaghung gloom
of St Columb's
    the brass eagle of
the lectern bearing
    the Sermon on the Mount
in its shoulders
    'A city that is
set on a hill
    cannot be hid'.

Columba's Derry!
   ledge of angels
radiant oakwood
   where the man-dove
knelt to master
   his fiery temper
exile chastened
   the bright candle
of the Uí Néill
   burns from Iona
lightens Scotland
   with beehive huts
glittering manuscripts
   but he remembers
his secret name
   'He who set his
back on Ireland'.

Lines of leaving
   lines of returning
the long estuary
   of Lough Foyle, a
ship motionless
   in wet darkness
mournfully hooting
   as a tender creeps
to carry passengers
   back to Ireland
a child of four
   this sad sea city
my landing place
   the loneliness of
Lir's white daughter's
   ice-crusted wings
forever spread
   at the harbour mouth.

Rearing westward
   the great sunroom
of Inis Eoghain
   coiling stones of
Aileach's hillfort
   higher than Tara
the Hy Niall
   dominating Uladh
the white cone
   of Sliabh Snacht
sorrow veiled
   the silent fjord
*is uaigneach Éire**
   as history's wind
plucks a dynasty
   from the ramparts
bids a rival
   settlement rise

London's Derry!
   METHOUGHT I SAW
DIDOE'S COLONY
   BUILDING OF CARTHAGE
culverin and saker
   line strong walls
but local chiefs
   come raging in
O'Cahan, O'Doherty
   (a Ferrara sword
his visiting card)
   a New Plantation
a new mythology
   Lundy slides
down a peartree
   as drum and fife
trill ORANJE BOVEN!

*Ireland is lonely

Lines of suffering
    lines of defeat
under the walls
    ghetto terraces
sharp pallor of
    unemployed shades
slope shouldered
    broken bottles
pubs and bookies
    red brick walls
Falls or Shankill
    Lecky or Fountain
love's alleyway
    message scrawled
Popehead: Tague
    my own name
hatred's synonym

But will the meek
    inherit the earth?
RELIGION POISONS US
    NORTH AND SOUTH.
A SPECIAL FORCE OF
    ANGELS WE'D NEED
TO PUT MANNERS ON US
    IF THE YOUNG WERE
HONEST, THEY'D ADMIT
    THEY DON'T HOLD
WITH THE HALF OF IT.
    THE SHOWBANDS
AND THE BORDER HALLS
    THAT'S THE STUFF
Said the guardian
    of the empty church
great siege windows
    shining behind us

Lines of protest
    lines of change
a drum beating
    across Berkeley
all that Spring
    invoking the new
Christ avatar
    of the Americas
running voices
    streets of Berlin
Paris, Chicago
    seismic waves
zigzagging through
    a faulty world

Overflowing from
    narrow streets
cramped fields
    a pressure rising
to match it
    tired marchers
nearing Burntollet
    young arms linked
banners poled high
    the baptism of
flying missiles
    spiked clubs
Law and Order's
    medieval armour
of glass shield
    and dangling baton

Lines of action
    lines of reaction
the white elephant
    of Stormont, Carson's
raised right claw
    a Protestant parliament
a Protestant people
    major this and
captain that and
    general nothing
the bland, pleasant
    face of mediocrity
confronting in horror
    its mirror image
bull-voiced bigotry

The emerging order
    of the poem invaded
by cries, protestations
    a people's pain
the defiant face
    of a young girl
campaigning against
    memory's mortmain
a blue banner
    lifting over a
broken province
    DRIVE YOUR PLOUGH
a yellow bulldozer
    raising the rubble
a humming factory
    a housing estate
hatreds sealed into
    a hygienic honeycomb

Lines of loss
    lines of energy
always changing
    always returning
A TIDE LIFTS
    THE RELIEF SHIP
OFF THE MUD
    OVER THE BOOM
the rough field
    of the universe
growing, changing
    a net of energies
crossing patterns
    weaving towards
a new order
    a new anarchy
always different
    always the same

Across the border
    a dead man
drives to school
    past the fort
at Greencastle
    a fury of love
for North, South
    eats his heart
on the far side
    a rocky promontory
his family name
    O'Cahan, O'Kane
my uncle watches
    sails upon Foyle
(a flock of swans)
    drives forward

# X

# THE WILD DOG ROSE

I. M. MINNIE KEARNEY

# 1

I go to say goodbye to the *cailleach,*
that terrible figure who haunted my childhood
but no longer harsh, a human being
merely, hurt by event.
                    The cottage,
circled by trees, weathered to admonitory
shapes of desolation by the mountain winds,
straggles into view. The rank thistles
and leathery bracken of untilled fields
stretch behind with — a final outcrop —
the hooped figure by the roadside,
its retinue of dogs
                    which give tongue
as I approach, with savage, whingeing cries
so that she slowly turns, a moving nest
of shawls and rags, to view, to stare
the stranger down.
                    And I feel again
that ancient awe, the terror of a child
before the great hooked nose, the cheeks
dewlapped with dirt, the staring blue
of the sunken eyes, the mottled claws
clutching a stick
                    but now hold
and return her gaze, to greet her,
as she greets me, in friendliness.
Memories have wrought reconciliation
between us, we talk in ease at last,
like old friends, lovers almost,
sharing secrets
                    of neighbours
she quarrelled with, who now lie
in Garvaghey graveyard, beyond all hatred;
of my family and hers, how she never married,
though a man came asking in her youth.
'You would be loath to leave your own,'
she sighs, 'and go among strangers' —
his parish ten miles off.
                         For sixty years
since, she has lived alone, in one place.
Obscurely honoured by such confidences,

I idle by the summer roadside, listening,
while the monologue falters, continues,
rehearsing the small events of her life.
The only true madness is loneliness,
the monotonous voice in the skull
that never stops
                        because never heard.


## 2


And there
where the dog rose shines in the hedge
she tells me a story so terrible
that I try to push it away,
my bones melting.
                        Late at night
a drunk came beating at her door
to break it in, the bolt snapping
from the soft wood, the thin mongrels
rushing to cut, but yelping as
he whirls with his farm boots
to crush their skulls.
                        In the darkness
they wrestle, two creatures crazed
with loneliness, the smell of the
decaying cottage in his nostrils
like a drug, his body heavy on hers,
the tasteless trunk of a seventy-year-
old virgin, which he rummages while
she battles for life
                        bony fingers
reaching desperately to push
against his bull neck. 'I prayed
to the Blessed Virgin herself
for help and after a time
I broke his grip.'
                        He rolls
to the floor, snores asleep,
while she cowers until dawn
and the dogs' whimpering starts
him awake, to lurch back across
the wet bog.

## 3

And still
the dog rose shines in the hedge.
Petals beaten wide by rain, it
sways slightly, at the tip of a
slender, tangled, arching branch
which, with her stick, she gathers
into us.
'The wild rose
is the only rose without thorns,'
she says, holding a wet blossom
for a second, in a hand knotted
as the knob of her stick.
'Whenever I see it, I remember
the Holy Mother of God and
all she suffered.'
Briefly
the air is strong with the smell
of that weak flower, offering
its crumbling yellow cup
and pale bleeding lips
fading to white
at the rim
of each bruised and heart-
shaped petal.

# EPILOGUE

*Driving South, we pass through Cavan,*
lakeside orchards in first bloom,
hawthorn with a surplice whiteness,
binding the small holdings of Monaghan.

A changing rural pattern means clack
of tractor for horse, sentinel shape
of silo, hum of milking machine:
the same from Ulster to the Ukraine.

Only a sentimentalist would wish
to see such degradation again:
heavy tasks from spring to harvest;
the sack-cloth pilgrimages under rain

to repair the slabbery gaps of winter
with the labourer hibernating
in his cottage for half the year
to greet the indignity of the Hiring Fair.

Fewer hands, bigger markets, larger farms.
Yet something mourns. The iron-ribbed
lamp flitting through the yard at dark,
the hissing froth, and fodder-scented warmth

of a wood-stalled byre, or leather thong
of flail curling in a barn, were part
of a world where action had been wrung
through painstaking years to ritual.

Acknowledged when the priest blessed
the green-tipped corn, or Protestant
lugged thick turnip, swollen marrow
to robe the kirk for Thanksgiving.

Palmer's softly lit Vale of Shoreham
commemorates it, or Chagall's lovers

floating above a childhood village
remote but friendly as Goldsmith's Auburn —

Our finally lost dream of man at home
in a rural setting! A giant hand,
as we pass by, reaches down
to grasp the fields we gazed upon.

Harsh landscape that haunts me,
well and stone, in the bleak moors of dream
with all my circling a failure to return
to what is already going
going
GONE

# THE GREAT CLOAK

*As my Province burns
I sing of love,
Hoping to give that fiery
Wheel a shove.*

I

SEARCH

## MOUNT VENUS

Forever the slim demon
elevates his claret cup
saying, there is but one life,
fill and drink up, while

over the villa'd suburbs
his careless laughter rings
before his snout vanishes
among a lady's earrings.

## THE HUNT

Chased beast, exultant huntress,
the same flood of hair.
I gripped you, you seized me.
In the battle, our limbs tangle forever.

But already impatient dawn breaks.
Blithe, surprised,
we refind our bodies.
So far, there is only somebody else.

*after André Frénaud*

## THE HUNTSMAN'S APOLOGY

You think I am brutal and without pity but at least I
execute cleanly because, like any true killer, I wish to
spare the victim. There are worse deaths. I have seen the
wounded bird trail her wing, and attract only the scaven-
ger. 'Help me', he croaks as he hops near. One dart of her
beak would settle him, for he is only a pale disciple of
Death, whom he follows at a distance. But she needs sym-
pathy and when he calls 'I am more unhappy than you'
her womanly heart revives and she takes him under her
broken wing. Her eyesight is poor and her senses dulled
but she feels an echo of lost happiness as he stirs against
her breast. She does not realise that he is quietly set-
tling down to his favourite meal of dying flesh, happily

enveloped in the smell of incipient putrefaction. The pain grows and spreads through her entire body until she cries aloud but it is too late to shake off his implanted beak. He grinds contentedly on and, as she falls aside, his bony head shoots up, like a scaldie out of a nest. His eye is alert, his veins coursing with another's blood and, for a brief moment, as he steps across the plain without looking back, his tread is firm as a conqueror's.

DO NOT DISTURB

A shaft rising towards,
or falling from, love.
Caressing glances, dart-
ing, possessive touches;
the porter's conspiracy,
distaste of the outraged.

That always strange moment
when the clothes peel away
(bark from an unknown tree)
with, not a blessing moon,
but a city's panelled skyline;
an early warning system

Before, disentangling,
through rain's soft swish,
the muted horns of taxis,
whirl of police or fire engine,
habitual sounds of loneliness
resume the mind again.

TRACKS

I

The vast bedroom
a hall of air,
our linked bodies
lying there.

II

As I turn to kiss
your long, black
hair, small breasts,
heat flares from
your fragrant skin,
your eyes widen as
deeper, more certain
and often, I enter
to search possession
of where your being
hides in flesh.

III

Behind our eyelids
a landscape opens,
a violet horizon
pilgrims labour across,
a sky of colours
that change, explode
a fantail of stars,
the mental lightning
of sex illuminating
the walls of the skull;
a floating pleasure dome.

IV

*I shall miss you*
creaks the mirror
into which the scene
shortly disappears:
the vast bedroom
a hall of air, the
tracks of our bodies
fading there, while
giggling maids push
a trolley of fresh
linen down the corridor.

My hand rests on
the table between
us. As we lean to
kiss, it tightens.

Then your long
fingernails stroke
& stroke the skin.
It slowly opens

so you can rest
your fragile fist,
trembling, a
balanced butterfly.

Love's pollen
lies lightly
on your skin;
a golden dust.
Let me brush
it with my wing!

## CAUGHT

A slight girl and easily got rid of:
He took his pleasure in an idle dance,
Laughed to hear her cry under him,
But woke to find his body in a trance.
Wherever he walked, he seemed to see
Her approaching figure, whoever spoke
He strained for echoes of her voice,
And, in a rage of loss, turned back
To where she slept, hands clasped on
Small breasts in a posture of defence.
Conqueror turned plaintiff, he tries
To uncurl them, to see long-lashed eyes
Turn slowly up, hear a meek voice say:
'Are you back, my love, back to stay?'

An ache, anger
thunder of a hurtling
waterfall in the ears:
in abrupt detail he sees
the room where she lays
her pale, soft body
under another's

her petal mouth
raised to absorb
his probing kiss
and hears her small voice
cry animal cries
in the hissing anguish
the release of

*my sweet one*
*my darling, my love*
until they fall apart
(Oh, the merciless creak
of jealousy's film)
in a wet calm
like flowers after rain.

After talking together
we move, as by a natural
progress, to make love.
Slant afternoon light

on the bed, the unlatched
window, scattered sheets
are part of a pattern
hastening towards memory

as you give yourself
to me with a cry of
joy, not hunger, while
I receive the gift

in ease, not raw desire
& all the superstructure
of the city outside —
twenty iron floors

of hotel dropping
to where the late sun
strikes the shield of
the lake, its chill towers —

are elements in a slowly
developing dream, a talisman
of calm, to invoke against
unease, to invoke against harm.

Ladies I have lain
        with in darkened rooms
sweet shudder of flesh
        behind shadowy blinds
long bars of light
        across tipped breasts
warm mounds of
        breathing sweetness
young flesh redolent
        of crumpled roses
the tender anxiety
        of the middle-aged
a hovering candle
        hiding blue veins
eloquent exhaustion
        watching light fade
as your drowsy partner
        drifts towards the
warm shores of sleep
        and you slowly awake
to confront again
        the alluring lie
of searching through
        another's pliant body
for something missing
        in your separate self
while profound night
        like a black swan
goes pluming past.

Love, a greeting
in the night, a
passing kindness,
wet leaf smell
of hair, skin

or a lifetime's
struggle to exchange
with the strange
thing inhabiting
a woman —
                        face,
breasts, buttocks,
the honey sac
of the cunt —

luring us to forget,
beget, a form of truth
or (the last rhyme
tolls its half tone)
an answer to death.

# II

# SEPARATION

Your *mistake,* my *mistake.*
*Small heads writhing,*
*a basket of snakes.*

The night is a great sleeping city
where the wind breathes. It has come
from far to our bed's safety, this June
midnight. You sleep, a hazel tree rustles,
I am led towards the borders of dream.
Comes that cry, nearing, disappearing,
a gleam fleeing through woods, or shades
some might say, which flit through hell.
(Of this midsummer night cry, how much
I could say, and of your gaze.) Though it is
only a bird called the screech owl, calling
from the depths of these suburban woods. And
already our bodies smell of the rankness
of the small hours, as under the warm skin
the bone pierces, while stars fade at street ends.

*after Philippe Jaccottet*

## LATE

I return late, on tiptoe.
Moonlight pours over the bed
and your still, sleeping head
reproving silently
my stealthy prowler's tread.

## DARKNESS

Against my knees
you lie, curled
like an animal
seeking warmth,
affection, the
caressing hand,
& speak sadly of

dreams you must
endure, left alone
at the mercy
of the powers
of night, when
darkness holds
all the land.

## CHILDLESS

Body
a garden summer ignores.

Body
a funeral where no one weeps.

Body
a husk without a kernel.

Body
a stone buried in earth.

**1**

I sing your pain
as best I can
        seek
like a gentle man
        to assume
the proffered blame.

But the pose breaks.
The sour facts remain.
        It takes two
to make or break
        a marriage.
*Unhood the falcon!*

**2**

*Pastourelle*

Hands on the pommel,
long dress trailing
over polished leather
riding boots, a spur
jutting from the heel,
& beneath, the bridle path,
strewn with rusty apples,
brown knobs of chestnut,
meadow saffron and acorn.

Then we were in the high
ribbed dark of the trees
where animals move stealth-
ily, coupling & killing,
while we talked nostalgically
of our lives, bedevilled
& betrayed by lost love —
the furious mole, tunnelling
near us his tiny kingdom —

& how slowly we had come
to where we wished each other
happiness, far and apart, as
a hawk circled the wood,
& a victim cried, the sound
of hooves rising & falling
upon bramble & fern, while
a thin growth of rain gathers
about us, like a cowl.

# 3

*Never*

In the gathering dark
I caress your head
as you thrash out
flat words of pain:
'There is no way back,
I can feel it happening;
we shall never be
what we were, again.'

*Never,* a solemn bell
tolling through
that darkening room
where I cradle your head,
only a glimmer left
in the high window
over what was once
our marriage bed.

# 4

*Refrain*

I sit in autumn sunlight
on a hotel terrace as I did

when our marriage had begun,
our public honeymoon,

try to unsnarl what went wrong,
shouldering all the blame,

but no chivalric mode,
courtesy's silent discipline

softens the pain
when something is ending

and the tearing begins:
'We shall never be

what we were, again.'
Old love's refrain.

As the thunderstorm
hovers over the car

your hand roves
over me, a frantic claw,

your mouth clamps
upon mine.

To kiss, in hunger
to kiss, in friendliness

not this salt
smart of anger and despair

an acrid salutation
bruising the lips.

After, in the dark
a voice in anger

by the roadside,
a worn car tyre

smouldering, a stench
of burning rubber.

In the white city of Evora, absence accosted me.
You were reading in bed, while I walked all night alone.
Were you worried about me, or drifting towards sleep?

I saw the temple of Diana, bone-white in the moonlight.
I made a private prayer to her, for strength to continue:
Not since convent days have I prayed so earnestly.

A dog came out of the shadows, brushed against my leg.
He followed me everywhere, pushing his nose into my hand.
Soon the cats appeared, little scraggy bundles of need.

There were more monuments, vivid as hallucinations.
Suddenly, a young man stepped out of the shadows:
I was not terrified, as I might have been at home.

Besides, he was smiling & gentle as you used to be.
'A kiss,' he pleads 'a kiss,' in soft Portuguese.
I quickened my step, but he padded behind me.

He looked so young, my heart went out to him.
I stopped in the shadows under the Cathedral.
We kissed, and the tears scalded my face.

We float in sunlight, inside the blue swimming pool, two fish in a glass bowl. And from your silence I realise that you would wish I were someone else. And that, at the same time as wishing me away, you are angry with me for causing that thought. My awareness of your desire, the thought of caresses which I cannot keep from imagining in detail (two bodies crawling over each other, enslimed with love), caresses I can no longer hope to receive, causes me more and more pain. And above all the despair when your eyes brighten at some mention of her, like a dreaming child. For you have always kept something of the eagerness of a child, looking forward to the next treat. But I have lost both faith and hope, and live on sufferance, an old tower crumbling by the water's edge.

## SEPARATION

Two fish float:

one slowly downstream
into the warm
currents of the known,

the other tugging
against the stream,
disconsolate twin,

the golden
marriage hook
tearing its throat.

Rue Daguerre, how we searched
till we found it! Beyond
the blunt-pawed lion of Denfert
to where, after the bustle
of an open-stalled market
you halt, before stooping
into a cobbled courtyard.

Symbol of the good life
this silence, each bend-
ing to his chosen task;
a Japanese farmer, tire-
less and polite, tending
a grafted cherry tree as
if it were his exiled self

which foamed to brief
and splendid blossom
each European spring.
The florist who made a
speciality of wreaths,
flower woven cartwheels
a cortège on his walls

smothered at Christmas
by fragrant limbs of fir.
The old woman stitching
moleskin sacks and bags
while her gross, gelded
cat dozed towards death
along its sunlit bench.

On Sunday mornings,
white canes racked,
two blind men played
the accordion, those
simple rippling tunes
that tore the heart:
'Sous les toits de Paris'

Or '*La vie en rose*',
setting for a shared
life, slowly broken,
wrenched, torn apart,
change driving its
blunt wedge through
what seemed permanent:

the cobbles uprooted,
the farmer beheaded
in a multiple accident,
a giant tower hulking
over the old market,
the traffic's roar
(waves grinding near

a littered shore)
while time whirls
faster and faster,
*j'attendrai tous
les jours*, a blind
accordion playing
to a funeral wreath.

L'ADIEU

I gathered this sprig of heather
The autumn is dead     remember
We shall never again see each other
Smell of time odour of heather
I wait for you     remember

*after Apollinaire*


NO MUSIC

I'll tell you a sore truth, little understood.
It's harder to leave, than to be left:
To stay, to leave, both sting wrong.

You will always have me to blame,
Can dream we might have sailed on;
From absence's rib, a warm fiction.

But I must recognise what I have done
And, if it fails, accept the burden
Of the harm done to you & another one.

To tear up old love by the roots,
To trample on past affections:
There is no music for so harsh a song.

## THE WANDERER

I stalk off through the morning fields.
The little house dwindles behind me;
If I glanced back I might not see it.

Shaking a handkerchief, she turns indoors.
For hours she will sit there, brooding,
Loathing me, yet wishing me home.

Along the cliffs I wander, hearing
The lean gulls cry. I hardly know where
I am bound, but I like the morning air.

I feel the sun warm on my shoulders.
My feet sink in earth, rough grass;
To be alone again, strange happiness!


## THE BLUE ROOM

Tired, turning, restless,
the insomniac feels the pulse
that feeds his body

pity for his past,
fear of the future,
his spirit beats

along his veins
a ceaseless, dervish dance
which defies oblivion.

Night a pit into
which he falls & falls
endlessly, his memories

a circle of hobbyhorses
grinding up and down
gross, grinning teeth

until dawn biting
its throat, a bird
starts its habitual

terrible, day-beginning cry.
The trees emerge from the stillness.
The raindrop bends the leaf.

I

'Dear one, no news from you so long.
I went and came back from the Alps,
I went and came back from the Vosges.
The boy you liked, the forester's son,
Who kept a yellow fox cub in the house
Now has a tame deer, which bumps wildly
Against the furniture, on bony stilts.
More news of shooting in the North.
Did you go to Enniskillen, as you said?
Lying alone at night, I see your body
Like Art O'Leary, that elegy you translated,
*Lying in a ditch before me, dead.*
The cherry tree is alight in the garden.
Come back to our little courtyard,' she said.

II

Again your lost, hurt voice;
'I hope this never happens you,
I wouldn't wish it upon anyone:
To live and dance in lonely fire,
To lie awake at night, listening
For a step that cannot come.
Of course I gave away the cats.
I found their lovesick cries
More than I could easily bear.
Remember our favourite Siamese?
The moment you entered the yard
He and I would both lift an ear.
Now he is dead, you are gone.
I sleep in the same room, alone.'

Habituée of darkness I have become.
Familiar of the secret feeding grounds
Where terror and dismay ceaselessly hatch,
Black forms curling and uncoiling;
The demons of the night feel like friends.

Something furry brushes along my arm,
A bat or screech owl hurtling by.
I clamber over stained rocks and find
The long gathered contents of our house
Swarming with decay, a filthied nest.

I came to where the eggs lay in the grass.
I watched them for a long time, warming them
With my swollen eyes. One after another
They chipped, and scraggy heads appeared;
The embryos of our unborn children.

They turn towards me, croaking 'Mother!'
I gather them up into my apron
But the shape of the house has fallen
And you are asleep by the water's edge:
A wind- and wave-picked skeleton.

## LIADAN LAMENTS CUIRITHIR

*from the Irish, 9th century*

Joyless
what I have done;
to torment my darling one.

But for fear
of the Lord of Heaven
he would lie with me here.

Not vain,
it seemed, our choice,
to seek Paradise through pain.

I am Liadan,
I loved Cuirithir
as truly as they say.

The short time
I passed with him
how sweet his company!

Forest trees
sighed music for us;
and the flaring blue of seas.

What folly
to turn him against me
whom I had treated most gently!

No whim
or scruple of mine
should have come between

Us, for above
all others, without shame
I declare him my heart's love.

A roaring flame
has consumed my heart:
I will not live without him.

In anger against
that strictness
in myself I wish
to ease, yet keep,

Dissolve that I
might the more
eagerly love;
learn to give.

As I have learnt
on occasions to weep
like a stricken animal
knowing nothing but

What was ailing me.
'But animals don't cry,'
you said, and I might
lightly have agreed

Had I not heard one
howl her companion
all night long, with
a more than human

Grief, an unconstrained,
teeth-baring lament,
into the untrespassable
realms of the dead.

*for Madeleine*

I

A light is burning late
in this Georgian Dublin street:
someone is leading our old lives!

And our black cat scampers again
through the wet grass of the convent garden
upon his masculine errands.

The pubs shut: a released bull,
Behan shoulders up the street,
topples into our basement, roaring 'John!'

A pony and donkey cropped flank
by flank under the trees opposite;
short neck up, long neck down,

as Nurse Mullen knelt by her bedside
to pray for her lost Mayo hills,
the bruised bodies of Easter Volunteers.

Animals, neighbours, treading the pattern
of one time and place into history,
like our early marriage, while

tall windows looked down upon us
from walls flushed light pink or salmon
watching and enduring succession.

## II

As I leave, you whisper,
'Don't betray our truth,'
and like a ghost dancer,
invoking a lost tribal strength,
I halt in tree-fed darkness

to summon back our past,
and celebrate a love that eased
so kindly, the dying bone,
enabling the spirit to sing
of old happiness, when alone.

## III

So put the leaves back on the tree,
put the tree back in the ground,
let Brendan trundle his corpse down
the street singing, like Molly Malone.

Let the black cat, tiny emissary
of our happiness, streak again
through the darkness, to fall soft
clawed into a landlord's dustbin.

Let Nurse Mullen take the last
train to Westport, and die upright
in her chair, facing a window
warm with the blue slopes of Nephin.

And let the pony and donkey come —
look, someone has left the gate open —
like hobbyhorses linked in
the slow motion of a dream

parading side by side, down
the length of Herbert Street,
rising and falling, lifting
their hooves through the moonlight.

# III

# ANCHOR

*Is maith an t-ancaire an t-iarta:*
*the hearth is a good anchor.*
— Old Irish Proverb

A MEETING

*from the Irish, 9th century*

The son of the King of the Moy
met a girl in green woods on mid-summer's day:
she gave him black fruit from thorns
& the full of his arms
of strawberries, where they lay.

A DREAM OF JULY

Silence
& damp night air
Flowing from the garden.

Like a young girl
Dissatisfied with
Her mythic burden
Ceres, corn goddess,
Mistress of summer,
Steps sure-footed over
The sweet smelling
Bundles of grass.
Her abundant body is
Compounded of honey
& gold, the spike
Of each small nipple
A wild strawberry —
Fulfilled in
Spite of herself
She exchanges with
The moon the pale
Gold disc of her face.

114

There is a secret room
of golden light where
everything — love, violence,
hatred is possible;
and, again, love.

Such intimacy of hand
and mind is achieved
under its healing light
that the shifting of
hands is a rite

like court music.
We barely know our
selves there though
it is what we always were —
most nakedly are —

and must remember
when we leave, re-
suming our habits
with our clothes:
work, phone, drive

through late traffic
changing gears with
the same gesture as
eased your snowbound
heart and flesh.

ALLEGIANCE

Beyond the village
herds browse peacefully
behind a barred wooden gate,
a warm Constable scene
of swirling shadows & silence;
a river's murmuring presence.

In their cumbrous circle
the huge stones stand,
completing the plain,
attending the dawn,
dew on granite, damp
on a sword blade.

Slowly, in moonlight
I drop to one knee,
solemn as a knight
obeying an ancient precept,
natural as cattle
stooping in river mist.

WALKING LATE

Walking late
we share night sounds
so delicate the heart misses
a beat to hear them:

shapes in the half-dark
where the deer feed or
rest, the radar of small
ears & horns still alert
under the glooming boles
of the great oaks
                    to unfold
their knees from the wet grass
with a single thrust & leap away
stiff-legged, in short, jagged
bursts as we approach
                    stars lining
our path through the woods

with a low coiling mist
over the nocturnal meadows
so that we seem to wade
through the filaments
of a giant silver web
the brain crevices of a cloud.

Bleached and white
as a fish's belly,
a road curves towards the city
which, with the paling dawn,

will surge towards activity again,
the bubble of the Four Courts
overruling the stagnant quays,
their ghostly Viking prows,

and the echoing archways,
tenebrous walls of the Liberties
where we briefly share a life

to which we must return
as we circle uncertainly
towards a home, your
smaller hand in mine.

SONG

Let me share with you
a glimpse of richness:
two swans startled me
turning low over the Lee,
looking for a nestling place.
I thought of us, our need
for a place to lay our heads;
our flight secret, unheralded.

By the curl and gleam
of water, my sadness
was washed away:
the air was bright
and clear as your forehead,
the linked swans
reached the wood:
*my love, come here to stay.*


WORKING DREAM

At the end of a manuscript
I was studying, a secret message.
A star, a honeycomb, a seashell,
The stately glory of a peacock's tail
Spiralled colour across the page
To end with a space between a lean I
And a warm and open-armed You.

An hour later, you were at the door;
I learnt the word that space was for.

BLESSING

A feel of warmth in this place.
In winter air, a scent of harvest.
No form of prayer is needed,
When by sudden grace attended.
Naturally, we fall from grace.
Mere humans, we forget what light
Led us, lonely, to this place.


WHEN THE WIND BLOWS

She sings a little
Off-key, for her
Coaxing lover
Who soothes her
To remember when
A huge figure —
The shadow of
Her father — fell
Across her crib,
Harshly shouting,
Startling the rattle
In her throat, and
When the bough
Breaks, she falls
Again, to feel
A different arm
Holding her up,
Safe and sound,
Above the void,
On the tree-top.

Like a team of horses,
manes lightstreaming,
we race together,
close, and separate.
Another night of sighs,
yet our love revives,
a flower in the morning

as, timid, uncertain,
you bring me small
conciliatory presents,
which you hold up
in your hands, face
pursed, like a squirrel,
waiting for me to smile.

Honeycomb of reconciliation:
thigh melting into thigh,
mouth into mouth, breast
turning against ribcage:
we make love as though
this small house were
a paradigm of the universe.


SUNSET

In Lough Leane
a queen went swimming;
a redgold salmon
flowed into her
at full of evening.

*from the* Féliré Aengus

## WAITING

Another day of dancing summer,
Evelyn kneels on a rock, breasts
Swollen by approaching motherhood,
Hair bleached by the sea winds
To a pale as honey gold, some
Generous natural image of the good.
Sails butterfly to her nakedness,
Surprised to spy through the haze
A curved figure, sleek as a mermaid,
Or bowsprit Venus, of smooth wood,
Courting the sun and not the shade,
Seagulls aureoling her bowed head,
Translucent as Wicklow river gold;
Source of my present guilt and pride.


## GOSSIP

Learn from the hare;
avoid too much notice,
crouch low, and quiet,
until the hunt passes.


## PROTEST

Awed, I bent in my gauze mask
to stroke your trembling hands
while our daughter was hauled
and forced into this breathing world.
The doctor stowed the forceps, red
as for a death, blood kin of birth,
and so I relived a simple truth;
we are born, as we die, reluctantly.
Your cries had stilled, anaesthetized,
and now only her protest was heard,
a raw fleshed morsel, briefly held
aloft, or mouthing furiously behind
her transparent plastic shield,
small paws kneading, kitten blind.

Smooth and long to swathe
a handsome woman's body,
a shape tall as a bell,
obedient to a fingernail.

Or to encompass her lover
as well, snug as flea deep
in featherbed, while their bodies
converse, on a green slope.

Or when the baby is born
to wrap the morsel tenderly
while beasts browse around them
naturally as in the peaceable kingdom.

CHILD

*for Úna*

A firefly gleams, then
fades upon your cheek.
Now you hide beneath
everything I write;
love's invisible ink,
heart's watermark.

## THE POINT

Rocks jagged in morning mist.
At intervals, the foghorn sounds
From the white lighthouse rock
Lonely as cow mourning her calf,
Groaning, belly deep, desperate.

I assisted at such failure once;
A night-long fight to save a calf
Born finally, with broken neck.
It flailed briefly on the straw,
A wide-eyed mother straddling it.

Listen carefully. This is different.
It sounds to guide, not lament.
When the defining light is powerless,
Ships hesitating down the strait
Hear its harsh voice as friendliness.

Upstairs my wife & daughter sleep.
Our two lives have separated now
But I would send my voice to yours
Cutting through the shrouding mist
Like some friendly signal in distress.

The fog is lifting, slowly.
Flag high, a new ship is entering.
The opposite shore unveils itself,
Bright in detail as a painting,
Alone, but equal to the morning.

PLEA

A dream of final ease, final understanding;
and then you make your staged entrance.

Medusa, eyes swollen, snake hair astray,
why will you not allow us some peace
before this long-sought house
your furies also clamour to destroy,
lashed by your divisive ecstasy?

Buckler bright, I stand ready to defy.


EDGE

Edenlike as your name
this sea's edge garden
where we rest, beneath
the clarity of a lighthouse.

To fly into risk,
attempt the dream,
cast off, as we have done,
requires true luck

who know ourselves
blessed to have found
between this harbour's arms
a sheltering home

where the vast
tides of the Atlantic
lift to caress
rose-coloured rocks.

So fate relents.
Hushed and calm,
safe and secret,
on the edge is best.

# THE DEAD KINGDOM

*El reino muerto vive todavia.* — Neruda

# I

# UPSTREAM

'There is no permanence. Do we build a house to stand
for ever, do we seal a contract to hold for all time? Do
brothers divide an inheritance to keep for ever, does the
flood-time of rivers endure? . . . When the judges come to-
gether, and the mother of destinies, together they decree
the fates of men. Life and death they allot but the day of
death they do not disclose.'
— The Book of Gilgamesh:
*Written down according to the original and collated in
the palace of Ashurbanipal, King of the World.*

*Northwards*, annually,
a journeying back,
the salmon's leap
& pull to the source:
my wife, from the shore
at Roche's Point, calls,
'John, come in, come home,
your mother is dead.'

We pull the currach
into shallow water,
haul her above tide
level, two sets of lean
insect legs stumbling
up the stony beach,
the curve of the boat
heavy on our napes
before we lift her
high on the trestles,
then store the long,
light oars, deliberately
neat and calm in crisis,
keeping the mind busy.

Under the lighthouse dome
the strangeness of Evelyn
weeping for someone
she has never known —
her child's grandmother —
while I stand, dry-eyed,
phoning and phoning a cousin
until, cursing, I turn
to feel his shadow loom
across the threshold.

Secret, lonely messages
along the air, older than
humming telephone wires,
blood talk, neglected
affinities of family,
antennae of instinct
reaching through space,
first intelligence.

(The night Ó Riada dies
a friend wakes up in
the South of France,
*feeling a great lightness,
a bird taking off.*)

Now Brendan sits silently
beside me in his car as
we drive through the long
monotony of our Midlands;
minor roads of memory
leading past a stone keep
stranded by history,
an ivy-strangled abbey
near his first home
where unemployed play
pitch and toss above
*a murmuring stream*
and a handball cracks
against tall concrete
while a ballad rises:
'Sweet Nelly Dean'!

My own memories as well:
wartime summers in this
sluggish, forgotten world,
chugging turf-fed trains,
Goldsmithian simplicities
of teacher and priest,
a tangled lane winding
to the hidden sweetness
of a whitewashed well
with, beyond the scringing
stile to the chapel,
wide, hedgeless fields
where I raced naked
under bent crab trees,
or pressed my body upon
the loam scented earth.

Triumphantly carrying home
trophies from the stream,
porringers of fresh water,
flecked with green weed,
in which minnows twisted
and turned in prison, or
stared out, enlarged
to gross-eyed monsters,
mouths kneading. . . .

A LAST GESTURE

*I. M. Mary O'Meara*

When his mother died,
her face calm, despite
great pain, she scorned
any false consolation —
'I'm done,' she repeated,
thinking only of the man
she had looked after
all their life, lying
in hospital, while she
drifted slowly down,
powerless to comfort,
no longer his woman,
resigning the human.

Before he was taken
away, he went again
to the well, laboriously
fetching her a can
of fresh spring water.
Her first food for days,
she found it tasted
sweet and chill, with
a trail and smell of
green seeping through
the acrid tinge
of metal. And praised
his last gesture,
saying, 'He was right:
its sweetness did me good.'

In the garden at Abbeylara
it was always summer,
bees fumbling the lilac,
the pink & white blossoms
of the flowering potatoes,
and here Uncle John comes,
fussily patting the drills
with the flat of his spade
while Aunt Mary reaches
over nestling hens, nettles,
to where soft raspberries
loosen on a spiky stem,
or gathers into her apron
tart pellets of currants,
gross, hairy gooseberries
to explode on the tongue.

In the house at Abbeylara
it was always busy & warm,
Uncle John bending down to
pat a terrier with eyebrows
as bushy as his own, or
crackling his newspaper,
'I saw Mick Collins once,
black-haired and laughing,
they shouldn't have shot him.'
Aunt Mary baking a scone
or rounding the crust on
a thick appletart while
the children cranked up
the great horned gramophone,
the tremulous melancholy
of Count McCormack's
silvery tongue soaring in
'Kathleen Mavourneen' or
*an old rustic bridge that*
*bends o'er a murmuring stream.*

Now they are both gone.
Months after their funerals
Brendan drives from Dublin,
to break, like a burglar,
into his old home, collect
stale documents, photographs.
The house smelt of neglect
and the garden was overrun;
crumbling unpicked berries
bending the tangled stems:
a small cleared realm
reverting to first chaos
as if they had never been.

The structure of process,
time's gullet devouring
parents whose children
are swallowed in turn,
families, houses, towns,
built or battered down,
only the earth and sky
unchanging in change,
everything else fragile
as a wild bird's wing;
bulldozer and butterfly,
dogrose and snowflake
climb the unending stair
into God's golden eye.

Each close in his own
world of sense & memory,
races, nations locked
in their dream of history,
only love or friendship,
an absorbing discipline
(the healing harmony
of music, painting, poem)
as swaying ropeladders
across fuming oblivion
while the globe turns,
and the stars turn, and
the great circles shine,
gold & silver,

  sun & moon.

GONE

So sing a song for
things that are gone,
minute and great,
celebrated, unknown.

The library of Alexandria,
the Fintona Horse Tram,
the royal city of Hué,
the pub of Phil Ryan.

Hovering fifty, I
have seen substantial things
hustled into oblivion:
castles, branchlines,

The Clogher Valley
railway bustling along
the hedges of Tyrone,
a Hornby toy train.

Tall walls of Dublin
dishonoured and torn;
Belfast's Victorian villas,
rose windows of the Crown;

Like the Great Forests
of Ireland, hacked down
to uphold the Jacobean
houses of London:

Chiding Spenser, I yet sing
of the goddess Mutability,
dark Lady of Process,
our devouring Queen.

*Master of royal decorum,*
*Great Lord of Babylon,*
*Excelling in the javelin,*
*Drawing of the long bow,*
*Charioteering, lion spearing;*

*All powers in the realm,*
*Both physical and mental,*
*Swift resolver of problems*
*With no apparent solution;*
*Who could read the tablets*
*In abstruse Sumerian. Sir,*

*Legendary as Nimrod of Nineveh,*
*Swift as Macedon's Alexander,*
*At twenty, the 'hegemon', benevolent*
*As the Buddha struck Ashoka,*
*Scholarly as Cormac of Cashel,*
*Wise as Justinian, brisk*
*As that codifying Corsican;*

*Who gave your craftsmen*
*Their dazzling freedom,*
*The hollow bronze lion*
*Crouched ready to spring,*
*The human headed scorpion;*

*I have seen your workroom,*
*Admired your quiet handling*
*Of some impossible problem,*
*Moving from point to point*

*Unperturbed by admiration,*
*So selflessly absorbed in*
*The task to hand, climbing*
*The ladder to defy oblivion:*

*Stand by us now, magister,*
*Staunch our deep wounds,*
*Light our dark island,*
*Heal our sad land.*

# II

## THIS NEUTRAL REALM

*Je dis ma mère. Et c'est à vous que je pense, O Maison!*
*Maison des beaux étés obscurs de mon enfance.*
— O. V. de Milocz (1877-1939)

*I cast a pebble down, to*
*Set the well's walls echoing.*
*As the meniscus resettles*
*I see a strange face form,*
*A wrinkled female face,*
*Sweeney's Hag of the Mill,*
*The guardian of the well,*
*Source of lost knowledge.*

Again, the unwinding road.

Across the Bog of Allen
(a sea of black peat,
our land's wet matrix)
showers mizzling until
over scant brush, necklaced
with raindrops, our reward:
a great cloak torn into
tatters of light, the warm
colours of heather deepened,
dyed to near violet, all
the air trembling, lambent —
slashes of rain, then sun
with small waves running in
on some reed-fringed island;
Loughs Gowna or Sheelin,
Derravarragh or Finea.

'Come back, Paddy Reilly'
to your changed world;
pyramids of turf stored
under glistening polythene:
chalk white power stations,
cleaned swathes of bog,
a carpet sucked clean!
Here the yellow machines
churned roots of bog-oak
like lopped antlers,
the sunken remnants
of the Great Forests
of Ireland, hoarse hunt-
ing horn of the Fianna,
the encumbered elk
crashing through branches,
a houndpack in full cry.

A nomadic world of
hunters and hunted;
beaten moons of gold,
a flash of lost silver,
figures coiling around
a bronze trumpet mouth:
a marginal civilisation
shading to the sound
of bells in monastic
sites, above the still
broadening Shannon,
or sheltered on some lake-
shore or wooded island:
from Derg to Devenish,
Loughs Gowna to Erne.

A slight fragrance revives:
cycling through the evening
to a dance in Gowna — Lake
of the Calf, source of Erne —
with one of the Caffreys.
Our carbide lamps wobbled
along the summer hedges, a
warm scent of hay & clover
as, after the dance, I kissed
my girl against a crumbling
churchyard wall.

       Our call
at a shebeen on the way back,
black pints by candlelight,
her leg warm against mine,
Barney grinning, with lewd
friendly jokes. I cycled
with her to buy strawberries
from the local big house,
fairy-tale Tullynally;
the Camelot of bogland,
its gothic turrets, stately
descending gardens, always
silvered with river mist.
A bay horse came trotting
down one of the paths, briskly
scattering the first leaves.
Bright spokes almost touch
as we push homewards,
silent dalliance of youth.

The Longford of my childhood,
a harebell lost in heather,
a rumble of donkey carts
across the Inny bridge
to the dwindling mounds
of hand slung turf, a
pony and trap rattling
past to market or Mass,
the view from the motte
of Granard over a tranquil
unrushed emptiness, a world
so torpid it woke only to
the tug of the long
church bell rope, the rasp
of a donkey's bray.

Time could stop here.

Hidden in the reeds,
a waterlogged boat,
stored by the Reillys.
We baled it first,
a hull full of green
dead water, clotted
with algae. Then slowly
we poled it, through
crackling walls of reed
with a single oar, to
where the current freed
itself, and the boat
accepts, rides, floats
on the oars' pull into
the brimming full heart
of the sunstruck lake.

A rod triangled against
a summer sky, life narrowed
to the plop of feeding
fish, the sudden flurry
of a bite, huge underjaw
of pike, or light, slim perch,
occasionally the thrash
of some larger fish:
the sun sinking as in
an old legend, *Sionnain*,
the grand-daughter of Lir,
drowned by angry salmon.
Where rats scamper, reeds
gleam like quicksilver,
we land, to gut and broil
our catch. Once, in a haul,
we found a ravenous pike;
inside its stomach, compact as
an embryo, an undigested perch.

We stretch in the grass
to water's lulling murmur.
A ghostly swan dips by;
Fionnuala, cold in her tragedy?
An immense stillness hangs
over Red Island, over
this deep, drowned land
of lobelia, marsh marigold,
a watery graveyard through
which the Inny wanders
its slow weed-choked way
to swell the Shannon.

The sky presses down
metal heavy, a helmet
banding the forehead,
subduing all brightness
to a brackish mist.
No branches stir, with
bird chirp, animal stealth.

We might be the first
to land on this shelf,
hauling up our long
hollowed boats, breaking
a clearing, with the
thick stroke of an axe
on wet wood, plumping

Fat stones, logs down
into the lake's stomach,
smoothing lichen to
floor rough huts of hide
or hacked wattle which
tangle in the wind
stretching & toughening.

The same skins supple
on our naked backs,
our brain a plait
of wet leaves, moss,
our eyes pinpoints
through drizzle, as
we crouched by a sunken

Cranny, breath tense
for the wary crackle
of hoof on grass,
an elk's span
of swaying branch;
the round soft eyes
of the musk ox.

Still, a violence lurks.
(Recall Blind Tadhg's name
for our land: Sword Land.)

Abruptly, a dragon's head
projects from the reeds,
the curling angry prow
of a Viking longship,
serrated wooden fangs
snapping the air, near
Clonmacnois, Bangor.
Bone biting axes, smoky
resinous torches, plunder
and burn, the flaring
pleasures of destruction!

Or iron knees protruding
below a metal heavy skirt,
the handle of a sword;
holding down Normandy,
hammering down Harold,
a harsh mastery harnessed
to an iron technology.

Their land-hungry prows
divide chill waters
for long years before
these sea-stained warriors
reconquer our land.

Rehearse Tadhg Dall's phrase
*Ferann cloidhimh, crioc Bhanba:*
Mountjoy's name for this land —
Ire Land: Sword Land?

*The great achievement of the South of Ireland*
*was to stand aside.*
                 — Louis MacNeice

Here, too, they defied Adolf.
A platoon of the L.D.F.
drilled in the parochial hall,
shouldering Lee Enfields.
A war intimate as a game,
miles better than Indians,
like the splendid manoeuvres
when the regular army came.

We defended Abbeylara
watching the Northern road —
signposts all gone —
from a girdered haybarn,
rifles at the ready,
with dummy cartridges,
until Southern Command
came behind our backs:
took over the town.

So I and my cousin
were captured, condemned
to spend a warm afternoon
incubating in an armoured car,
peering through slits,
fingering the intricacy
of a mounted Bren gun.

So we learnt to defend
this neutral realm,
each holiday summer,
against all comers,
including the Allies
if they dared to cross over
(Hitler being frightened).
Eire's most somnolent time
while, at home, invasion
forces risked chilling seas
to assemble in Ulster.

Already seen through
the stereoscopic lens
of a solitary childhood,
our divided allegiances;
a mock and a real war:
Spitfire and Messerschmitt
twinned in fire, Shermans
lumbering through our hedges,
ungainly as dinosaurs, while
the South marched its toy
soldiers along the sideline.


THE MUSIC BOX

And now, the road towards Cavan.
Each year, we left you down
by the roadside, Mary Mulvey,
to seek out old relations.
We waited, as you hobbled
away, up that summer boreen.

Mary lived in the leaning
cottage, beside the old well
she strove to keep clean,
bending to skin dead leaves
and insects; ageing guardian
whom we found so frightening

Huddled on the leather seats
of Uncle John's Tin Lizzie
away from your sour, black
shawls, clacking rosary, not
your bag of peppermints, which
we devoured, thoughtlessly.

'Maria Marunkey', our hurtful
childish name for your strange
shape, suffering age, its shame
that hooped your back, cramped
and horrible as some toothy witch.
We clattered stones on your roof

Or hunkered whispering past
your half-door, malefic dwarfs,
to startle your curtained silence
with shouts, coarse as farts:
'Maria Marunkey married a donkey.'
The latch stirs; we scatter, bravely.

Blessedly, you could barely hear,
or begged us in, with further sweets
or gifts, to share your secret.
Nudging, we thronged around
as you laboriously wound —
more creakingly each year —

The magic music box, resurrected
from camphored lace, which ground
out such light, regular sounds,
thawing ice, tinkling raindrops,
a small figure on its rosewood top
twirling slowly, tireless dancer.

By its grace, I still remember
you, Mary Mulvey, hobbling along
a summer lane, bent over the well
or shuffling into your cottage,
its gable sideways, like yourself.
Your visits to the home place

To see old friends and neighbours
stopped one year when you were
too crippled to move, and besides;
'There's no one left up there.
They've all died off.' A silver
dancer stops. Silent. Motionless.

I

*The well dreams;*
*liquid bubbles.*

*Or it stirs*
*as a water spider skitters across;*
*a skinny legged dancer.*

*Sometimes, a gross interruption;*
*a stone plumps in.*
*That takes a while to absorb,*
*to digest, much groaning*
*and commotion in the well's stomach*
*before it can proffer again*
*an almost sleek surface.*

*Even a pebble disturbs*
*that tremor laden meniscus,*
*that implicit shivering.*
*They sink towards the floor,*
*the basement of quiet,*
*settle into a small mosaic.*

*And the single eye*
*of the well dreams on,*
*a silent cyclops.*

II

*People are different.*
*They live outside, insist*
*in their world of agitation.*
*A man comes by himself,*
*singing or in silence,*
*and hauls up his bucket slowly —*
*an act of meditation —*
*or jerks it up angrily,*
*like lifting a skin,*
*sweeping a circle*
*right through his own reflection.*

III

*And the well recomposes itself.*

*Crowds arrive annually, on pilgrimage.*
*Votive offerings adorn the bushes;*
*a child's rattle, hanging silent*
*(except when the wind shifts it)*
*a rag fluttering like a pennant.*

*Or a tarnished coin is thrown in,*
*sinking soundlessly to the bottom.*
*Water's slow alchemy washes it clean:*
*a queen of the realm, made virgin again.*

IV

*Birds chatter above it.*
*They are the well's principal distraction,*
*swaying at the end of branches,*
*singing and swaying, darting excitement*
*of courting and nesting,*
*fending for the next brood,*
*who still seem the same robin,*
*thrush, blackbird or wren.*

*The trees stay silent.*
*The storms speak through them.*
*Then the leaves come sailing down,*
*sharp green or yellow,*
*betraying the seasons,*
*till a flashing shield of ice*
*forms over the well's single eye:*
*the year's final gift,*
*a static transparence.*

V

*But a well has its secret.*
*Under drifting leaves,*
*dormant stones around*
*the whitewashed wall,*
*the unpredictable ballet*
*of waterbugs, insects,*

*There the wellhead pulses,*
*little more than a tremor,*
*a flickering quiver,*
*spasms of silence;*
*small intensities of mirth,*
*the hidden laughter of earth.*

# III

# THE BLACK PIG

*I have arranged to increase the animosity
between Orangemen and the United Irish.
Upon that animosity depends the safety of
the centre counties of the North . . .*
— General Knox, *March 1797*

Ballinagh, its flat, main street;
that sudden, sharp turn North.
Nearby, a ridge of the Dunchaladh,
the Black Pig's Dyke, or Race, —
the ancient frontier of Uladh.

Straying through a Breton forest
once, I heard a fierce scrabbling,
saw his blunt snout when,
with lowered tusks, a wild boar
ignored me, bustling past.

And can still believe in
some mythic bristled beast
flared nostrils, red in anger,
who first threw up, where North
crosses South, our bloody border.

(Or some burrowing Worm
slithering through the earth
from Ballinagh to Garrison,
a serpent's hiss between
old Uladh and Ireland.)

And now he races forever,
a lonely fearsome creature,
furrowing a trough we may
never fill, the ancient guardian
of these earthworks of anger.

The farther North you travel, the colder it gets.
Take that border county of which no one speaks.
Look at the straggly length of its capital town:
the bleakness after a fair, cattle beaten home.
The only beauty nearby is a small glacial lake
sheltering between drumlin moons of mountains.
In winter it is completely frozen over, reeds
bayonet sharp, under a low, comfortless sky.
Near the middle there is a sluggish channel
where a stray current tugs to free itself.
The solitary pair of swans who haunt the lake
have found it out, and come zigzagging,
holding their breasts aloof from the jagged
edges of large pale mirrors of ice.

That wavering needle
pointing always North.
Approaching our Border
why does my gorge rise?
I crossed it how often
as a boy, on the way
to my summer holidays,
and beyond Aughnacloy
felt a sense of freedom
following the rough roads
through Cavan, Monaghan,
greeted at a lakeside orchard
where we stopped to buy
apples, Bramley seedlings,
Beauty of Bath, with
its minute bloodstains.

But by the sand-bagged
barracks of Rosslea, Derrylin
the route is different.
Wearing years later
I go North again and again —
Express bus from Dublin,
long car ride from Munster —
to visit my mother when
she wastes away slowly in
a hospital in Enniskillen:
learn the bitter lesson
of that lost finger of land
from Swanlinbar to Blacklion

Under Quilca Mountain
inching the car across
a half-bombed bridge,
trespassing, zigzagging
over potholed roads, post-
boxes, now green, now red,
alternately halted by British
patrols, unarmed *gardaí*,
signs in Irish and English,
both bullet-pierced, into
that shadowy territory
where motives fail, where
love fights against death,
good falters before evil.

Near here, he stood,
the Stooped One,
lord of darkness,
drinker of blood,
eater of the young,
king of the void,
The Golden Stone.

But are such visions
of an abstract evil
an evasive fiction:
the malignant Crom
but the warming sun,
his attendant stones
the whirling seasons?

The evil sprang from
our own harsh hearts:
thronged inhabitants
of this turning world,
cramped into a corner,
labelled by legend,
Ulster or Northern Ireland.

Source of such malevolence,
a long-nurtured bitterness.
No Nordic family feud,
arm & thighbone scattered
(*the ravens have gorged
on a surfeit of human flesh*)
but wise imperial policy

Hurling the small peoples
against each other, Orange
Order against Defender,
neighbour against neighbour,
blind rituals of violence,
our homely Ulster swollen
to a Plain of Blood.

THE WEB OF MAN (A CURSE)

*from the old Norse, 11th century*

> A rainfall of blood
> from the clouded web,
> the broad loom
> of man slaughter!
> Slate armour grey
> the web of our fate
> is long being woven:
> the furies cross it
> with threads of crimson.
>
> The warp, the weft
> are of human entrails.
> Their severed heads
> dangle as weights,
> blood dark swords
> are spiralling rods.
> The arrows clatter
> as the furies weave
> the web of battle.
>
> The land of Ireland
> will suffer a grief
> that will never heal.
> Men, as yet unknown,
> who now dwell upon
> wind-lashed headlands
> will hold the nation.
> The web is now woven:
> the battlefield crimson.

Sing a song for the broken
towns of old Tyrone:
Omagh, Dungannon, Strabane,
jagged walls and windows,
slowly falling down.

Sing a song for the homes
or owners that were here today
and tomorrow are gone;
Irish Street in Dungannon,
my friend, Jim Devlin.

Sing a song for the people,
so grimly holding on,
Protestant and Catholic, fingered
at teabreak, shot inside their home:
the iron circle of retaliation.

Sing a song for the creaking branch
they find themselves upon,
hollow from top to bottom,
the stricken limb of Ulster,
slowly blown down.

Sing an end to sectarianism,
Fenian and Free Presbyterian,
the punishment slowly grown
more monstrous than the crime,
an enormous seeping bloodstain.

Sing our forlorn hope then —
the great Cross of Verdun,
Belfast's Tower on the Somme —
signs raised over bloody ground
that two crazed peoples make an end.

DEITIES

*From our needs*
*we create them:*
*the lean Christ*
*we help to press,*
*impale upon the*
*timbered cross*

*expertly. See us*
*plant the nails,*
*marvel at his*
*blood-streaked*
*but accepting face,*

*and the gentle*
*smile of Gautama,*
*absolving evil,*
*the lusts, frail*
*terrors of the flesh.*

*Like St Francis*
*he gives away*
*property right*
*and left until*
*a calm shines*

*over our broken*
*lives, tangled*
*wills, bitter*
*battlefields of*
*society and self.*

*But the old gods*
*surged from earth,*
*air, fire, water:*
*radiant Hermes glid-*
*ing the light shafts;*

*black extensions*
*of earth's under-*
*ground empery of*
*roots and rocks:*
*O gloomy Dis!*

Or from a headland
the sea's power —
a trident finning
the furious waves —
all hail, Poseidon!

While the luxuriant
wind caressed grain
of high summer
murmurs of warmth:
O sweet Ceres!

∽

God or goddess,
they distributed
their favours in
the battle's heat
they stoke so well —

tripping Cuchulainn,
clouding Achilles
in a psychic confusion
of light and dark:
Balor or Polyphemus,

until Ulysses or
Lugh props open
the baleful eyelid,
lunges home with
the burning stake.

Abandons, wisdoms;
left to himself,
stripped of creed,
man still faces
the old powers:

violence fuming
from some crater,
knows his own dark,
scales his light,
steers his craft.

# IV

# THE SILVER FLASK

*Everything that is not suffered
to the end and finally concluded,
recurs, and the same sorrows
are undergone.*
— Hermann Hesse

A glimmer of light on
the turning ocean floor;
the moon's white disc
waxing and waning, as
a woman waits, a womb
waits, for the leap
of conception, here in
Ireland, or alien Brooklyn.
The gravity of our child
growing in Evelyn's womb,
unacknowledged, unknown,
while my forsaken mother
wastes glumly away in
a new aseptic hospital
high above Enniskillen;
an exhausted woman, and
a child who will resemble
her, spirits exchanging
in familial communion.

What lonely outcry equals
such a flaring mystery?
Consumed by pain, still
her motherly concern,
enquiring how I had come
so far North again —
just beyond Aughnacloy,
the girdered skeleton
of a burnt-out Express
I had rushed to catch.
And probing delicately —
where is Madeleine?
so that I might have
sought to explain;
but gentleness forbade.
Should one disturb
the dreams of the old;
her whole life dominated
by an antique code?

Before Aughnacloy, they are ordered to dismount.
'For God and Ulster', he shouts, waving a pistol,
a shadow in the twilight, daft as Don Quixote,
except for that gun stuck in the driver's throat
and brother shadow, sullen in his anorak.
A forced comradeship of passengers trembles
by the sleety roadside, attending sudden death.
Assistant shadow sprinkles petrol leisurely
over the back and sides of the Derry Express
while chief shadow asks them to remove their boots,
the classic ritual before a mass execution.
Lucky this time, they are spared, warned off
to tramp behind the driver two miles in the snow
not daring, like Lot's wife, to look for the glow
of their former bus, warming the hedges:
their only casualty, thin socks worn through.

INTIMACY

'Mother, mother,' I whisper,
over the years we had won
to a sweet intimacy together.
She would come with me often
to Fintona's first picturehouse,
rigged out like a girlfriend
in her evening finery, snug
in the best seats, munching
soft centred chocolates. Naturally
we chose romances, Sir Laurence
stalking the cliffs in *Rebecca*,
Leslie Howard defending the South,
courteous through cannonsmoke,
and I thought I might bring her
to some sad story of Brooklyn,
the bridge's white mirage shining
over broken lives like her own,
but she wept, and dabbed her eyes;
'I hate films about real life.'

Melancholy destiny, indeed.
Young love, then long separation.
After our drive across Ireland,
my father stood in the kitchen,
surrounded by his grown sons
and the wife he had not seen
for almost two decades, spirit
glass in hand, singing 'Slievenamon'
or *Molly Bawn, why leave me pining*,
his eyes straying in strangeness
to where she sat, with folded
hands, grey hair, aged face,
*Alone, all alone by the wave*
*washed strand*, still his Molly Bawn,
wrought by time to a mournful crone.

Six years later, he was gone,
*to a fairer world than this*,
and we sat in television darkness,
searching from channel to channel
while the badmen came riding in,
guns glinting in the prairie sun,
or the pretty nurse fell in love
with the subtle handed surgeon
as the emergency was wheeled in —
*tho' lonely my life flows on* —
and she laughed, reaching down
for the brandy by her side, or
excitedly darting snuff, dust
settling on her apron. . . .


MOLLY BAWN

Short hair crimped
with curling tongs,
the belle of Fintona's
*Cumann na mBan,*
haranguing the throng
upon Liskey Brae,
singing rebel songs
on the beach at Bundoran,
knocking the helmet

off a big policeman
with your parasol;
a true Fenian!

His Irish Molly
Father called you,
your courtship & wedding
to the sound of marching.
Remember your honeymoon
in troubled Dublin:
a brattle of gunfire
as our pious father
hurries to early Mass
in Newman's Church —
to thank God perhaps? —
the morning after.

Then the long trek
to solace your brothers:
Frank, a medical student
in the Kevin Barry regiment,
interned in Ballykinlar,
Tom, down in the Curragh.
Sprung, after the Treaty,
they serve as officers in
the new Free State Army,
their first national duty
to hunt down old comrades,
split by the Treaty.

Absurdity leads to atrocity;
deserters, after Ballyseedy.
Emigrating anywhere, suburban
England, prohibition Brooklyn,
the embittered diaspora of
dispossessed Northern Republicans
scorning their State Pensions;
a real lost generation. Then
my mother follows her husband,
my future father, off to the New
World, making sure to land in
good time for the Depression!

My mother,
my mother's memories
of America;
a muddy cup
she refused to drink.

His landlady didn't know
my father was married
so who was the woman
landed on the doorstep
with grown sons

my elder brothers
lonely & lost
Father staggers back
from the speakeasy
for his stage entrance;

the whole scene as
played by Boucicault
or Eugene O'Neill:
the shattering of
that early dream

but that didn't
lessen the anguish,
soften the pain, so
she laid into him
with the frying pan

till he caught her
by the two wrists,
'Molly, my love, if
you go on like this
you'll do yourself harm.'

And warmly under
a crumbling brownstone
roof in Brooklyn
to the clatter of
garbage cans

like a loving man
my father leant
on the joystick
& they were reconciled,
made another child,

a third son who
beats out this song
to celebrate the odours
that bubbled up
so rank & strong

from that muddy cup
my mother refused
to drink but kept
wrinkling her nose
in souvenir of

*(cops and robbers,*
*cigarstore Indians*
*& coal black niggers,*
*bathtub gin and*
*Jewish neighbours).*

Decades after
she had returned
to the hilly town
where she had been born,
a mother cat,

intent on safety,
dragging her first
batch of kittens back
to the familiar womb-warm
basket of home

(all but the runt
left to be fostered
in Garvaghey,
seven miles away;
her husband's old home).

Christmas in Brooklyn,
the old El flashes by.
A man plods along pulling
his three sons on a sleigh;
soon his whole family
will vanish away.

My long lost father
trudging home through
this strange, cold city,
its whirling snows,
unemployed and angry,
living off charity.

Finding a home only
in brother John's speakeasy.
Beneath the stoup
a flare of revelry.
And yet you found time
to croon to your last son.

Dear Father, a gracenote.
That Christmas, you did
find a job, guarding a
hole in the Navy Yard.
Elated, you celebrated
so well, you fell in.

Not a model father.
'I was only happy
when I was drunk,'
you said, years later,
building a fire in
a room I was working in.

Still, you soldiered on
all those years alone in
a Brooklyn boarding house
without your family
until the job was done;
and then limped home.

A small sad man with a hat
he came through the Customs at Cobh
carrying a roped suitcase and
something in me began to contract

but also to expand. We stood,
his grown sons, seeking for words
which under the clouding mist
turn to clumsy, laughing gestures.

At the mouth of the harbour lay
the squat shape of the liner
hooting farewell, with the waves
striking against Spike Island's grey.

We drove across Ireland that day,
lush river valleys of Cork, russet
of the Central Plain, landscapes
exotic to us Northerners, halting

only in a snug beyond Athlone
to hear a broadcast I had done.
How strange in that cramped room
my disembodied voice, the silence

after, as we looked at each other!
Slowly our eyes managed recognition.
'Not bad,' he said, and raised his glass:
Father and son at ease, at last.

## THE SILVER FLASK

Sweet, though short, our
hours as a family together.
Driving across dark mountains
to Midnight Mass in Fivemiletown,
lights coming up in the valleys
as in the days of Carleton.

Tussocks of heather brown
in the headlights; our mother
stowed in the back, a tartan
rug wrapped round her knees,
patiently listening as Father sang,
and the silver flask went round.

Chorus after chorus of the 'Adoremus'
to shorten the road before us,
till *we see amidst the winter's snows*
the festive lights of the small town
and from the choirloft an organ booms
*angels we have heard on high*, with

my father joining warmly in,
his broken tenor soaring, faltering,
a legend in dim bars of Brooklyn
(that sacramental moment of stillness
among exiled, disgruntled men)
now raised vehemently once again

in the valleys he had sprung from,
startling the stiff congregation
with fierce blasts of song, while
our mother sat silent beside him,
sad but proud, an unaccustomed
blush mantling her wan countenance.

Then driving slowly home,
tongues crossed with the Communion
wafer, snowflakes melting in
the car's hungry headlights,
till we reach the warm kitchen
and the spirits round again.

The family circle briefly restored
nearly twenty lonely years after
that last Christmas in Brooklyn,
under the same tinsel of decorations
so carefully hoarded by our mother
in the cabin trunk of a Cunard liner.

*I. M. James Montague*

We stand together
on the windy platform;
how sharp the rails
running out of sight
through the wet fields!

Carnew, the station master,
is peering over
his frosted window:
the hand of the signal
points down.

Crowned with churns
a cart creaks up the
incline of Main Street
to the sliding doors
of the Co-Op.

A smell of coal,
the train is coming . . .
You climb slowly in,
propped by my hand to
a seat, back to the engine,

and we leave, waving
a plume of black smoke
over the rushy meadows,
small hills and hidden villages —
Beragh, Carrickmore,

Pomeroy, Fintona —
placenames that sigh
like a pressed melodeon
across this forgotten
Northern landscape.

What a view he has
of our town, riding
inland, the seagull!

Rows of shining roofs
and cars, the dome of
a church, or a bald-

headed farmer, and
a thousand gutters
flowing under the

black assembly
of chimneys! If
he misses anything

it might be history
(the ivy-strangled
O'Neill Tower only

a warm shelter to
come to roost if
crows don't land

first, squabbling;
and a Planter's
late Georgian house

with its artificial
lake, and avenue of
poplars, less than

the green cloth of
our golf-course where
fat worms hide from

the sensible shoes
of lady golfers).
Or religion. He may

not recognise who
is driving to Mass
with his army of

freckled children —
my second brother —
or hear Eustace

hammer and plane
a new coffin for
an old citizen,

swearing there is
no one God as the
chips fly downward!

*He would be lost,*
*my seagull, to see*
*why the names on*

*one side of the street*
*(MacAteer, Carney)*
*are Irish and ours*

*and the names across*
*(Carnew, MacCrea)*
*are British and theirs*

*but he would understand*
*the charred, sad stump*
*of the factory chimney*

*which will never burn*
*his tail feathers as*
*he perches on it*

*and if a procession,*
*Orange or Hibernian,*
*came stepping through*

*he would hear the*
*same thin, scrannel*
*note, under the drums.*

*And when my mother*
*pokes her nose out*
*once, up and down*

*the narrow street,*
*and retires inside,*
*like the lady in*

*the weather clock,*
*he might well see*
*her point. There are*

*few pickings here,*
*for a seagull, so*
*far inland. A last*

*salute on the flag*
*pole of the British*
*Legion hut, and he*

*flaps away, the*
*small town sinking*
*into its caul*

*of wet, too well-*
*hedged, hillocky*
*Tyrone grassland.*

173

# V

# A FLOWERING ABSENCE

> *. . . I am re-begot*
> *Of absence, darkness, death; things which are not.*
>                                         — John Donne

When the wall between her and ghost
Wears thin, then snuff, spittoon,
Soothing drink cannot restrain:
She ransacks the empty house.
The latch creaks with the voice
Of a husband, the crab of death
Set in his bowels, even the soft moon
Caught in the bathroom window
Is a grieving woman, her mother
Searching for home in the Asylum.
What awaits, she no longer fears
As dawn paints in the few trees
Of her landscape, a rusty shed
And garden. Today grandchildren
Call, but what has she to say
To the buoyant living, who may
Raise family secrets with the dead?


## PROCESSION

*I. M. Grandmother Hannah Carney*

Hawk nose, snuff-stained apron;
I stand beside you again in
the gloom of your hallway
peering up & down Fintona's
cattle-stained Main Street
some thronged fairday evening.

As you ramble on, like someone
sick or drunk, confessing to
a stranger in a bar, or train;
ignoring my small years while
you spell out your restless pain,
mourn a tormented lifetime.

Frank, your pride, eldest boy,
interrogated again and again,
arrested in your warm kitchen,
bayonets and British voices
bullying him abruptly away
to the barbed wire, the tin

huts of Ballykinlar, model
for Long Kesh, Magilligan.
Your youngest son, Tom, then
drills in the old bandroom
to follow him; soon lands
himself into the Curragh prison.

Released, your two internees
were met at the railway station,
cheered and chaired home
with a torchlight procession:
but one half of the town
held its blinds grimly down.

Still hatred and division
stain that narrow acre
from which you sprang.
A half century later
the same black dreams
return to plague your daughter,
their sister, my mother.

A Paisleyite meeting
blared outside her window.
A military helicopter
hovered over the hospital,
a maleficent spider. Her
dying nightmares were of her
sons seized by soldiers!

Across the rough, small hills
of your country girlhood —
the untamed territory of
the Barr, Brougher Mountain —
we brought your daughter home,
yellow car beams streaming;
a torchlight procession.

*Northwards stream the wild*
*geese, through the long Polar*
*night (the bewildered cries*
*of the newly dead, shocked*
*spirits hurled out of life)*
*with the slow flap of wide*
*thunderous wings lured by*
*an ultimate coldness, that*
*magnetic needle wavering,*
*trembling always North.*

On the funeral morning
I wrench from dark dream
to find my cousin's arm
looped loosely over mine.
We dress and drive down
the seven long miles that
separated me from mother
and brother, Montague
from Carney, fading farm
from stagnant small town.

In my hostile imagination
chill rain always beats down
on these small grey houses,
only gay on market days,
the ballad-singer's voice
raised in rough song:
*On top of Old Smokey,*
*all covered with snow,*
*I lost my own true love*
*by courting too slow.*

A stranded community,
haunted by old terrors,
the Dromore murders;
neither Irish, nor British,
its natural hinterland
severed by the border:
doleful men lounging
along the station wall;
Golfcourse and Carnival,
the effort to seem normal.

Here my mother lived
where her mother lived
before her, endlessly
toiling narrow stairs,
endlessly raking over
the cold ashes of
her neighbours' foibles,
marginally living, and
obsessed with dying,
now finally managed.

The ceremony, soon over;
no ritual graces the event,
a lifeless modern funeral
without music or song,
to lament the dead, or
ease the living. No piper
struts, or kneels down,
with swelling resonance,
no slow fiddle lifts, to
sweeten our burden.

A few clods clump down
and now she lies again
with our father, near
her own mother, while
across the fresh grave
an upright relative tries
hard to slight me, but
I want no truck with
this narrowing world
of bigotry and anger.

Each death is our own:
a child of seven, as
dawn drew in, I would
lie awake, singing &
sighing to myself, *I*
*am I, and I must die;*
recognising the self as
I feared the end of it:
the spirit fretting in-
side the body's casket.

Consciousness, a firefly
sparkling with cognition,
living through a thousand
minor deaths, as the atoms
of the body decay, separate,
to be endlessly rewoven,
endlessly reborn, my body
of seven years ago, shed;
this final death, a freedom;
a light battling through cloud.

*By whistling you could*
*bring them nearer —*
*or so I was often told.*
*A magnetic storm of*
*particles, a sperm*
*shower of the sun,*
*violent sounds haunting*
*lost Polar expeditions —*
*our sky's virid necklace,*
*the Northern Lights.*

How can one make an absence flower,
lure a desert to sudden bloom?
Taut with terror, I rehearse a time
when I was taken from a sick room:
as before from your flayed womb.

And given away to be fostered
wherever charity could afford.
I came back, lichened with sores,
from the care of still poorer
immigrants, new washed from the hold.

I bless their unrecorded names,
whose need was greater than mine,
wet nurses from tenement darkness
giving suck for a time,
because their milk was plentiful

Or their own children gone.
They were the first to succour
that still terrible thirst of mine,
a thirst for love and knowledge,
to learn something of that time

Of confusion, poverty, absence.
Year by year, I track it down
intent for a hint of evidence,
seeking to manage the pain —
how a mother gave away her son.

I took the subway to the hospital
in darkest Brooklyn, to call
on the old nun who nursed you
through the travail of my birth
to come on another cold trail.

'Sister Virgilius, how strange!
She died, just before you came.
She was delirious, rambling of all
her old patients; she could well
have remembered your mother's name.'

Around the bulk of St Catherine's
another wild, raunchier Brooklyn:
as tough a territory as I've known,
strutting young Puerto Rican hoods,
flash of blade, of bicycle chain.

Mother, my birth was the death
of your love life, the last man
to flutter near your tender womb:
a neonlit bar sign winks off & on,
*motherfucka, thass your name.*

There is an absence, real as presence.
In the mornings I hear my daughter
chuckle, with runs of sudden joy.
Hurt, she rushes to her mother,
as I never could, a whining boy.

All roads wind backwards to it.
An unwanted child, a primal hurt.
I caught fever on the big boat
that brought us away from America —
away from my lost parents.

Surely my father loved me,
teaching me to croon, *Ragtime Cowboy
Joe, swaying in his saddle
as he sings,* as he did, drunkenly
dropping in from the speakeasy.

So I found myself shipped back
to his home, in an older country,
transported to a previous century,
where his sisters restored me,
natural love flowering around me.

And the hurt ran briefly underground
to break out in a schoolroom
where I was taunted by a mistress
who hunted me publicly down
to near speechlessness.

'So this is our brightest infant?
Where did he get that outlandish accent?
What do you expect, with no parents,
sent back from some American slum:
none of you are to speak like him!'

Stammer, impediment, stutter:
she had found my lode of shame,
and soon I could no longer utter
those magical words I had begun
to love, to dolphin delight in.

And not for two stumbling decades
would I manage to speak straight again.
Grounded for the second time
my tongue became a rusted hinge
until the sweet oils of poetry

eased it and grace flooded in.


THE LOCKET

Sing a last song
for the lady who has gone,
fertile source of guilt and pain.
*The worst birth in the annals of Brooklyn*,
that was my cue to come on,
my first claim to fame.

Naturally, she longed for a girl,
and all my infant curls of brown
couldn't excuse my double blunder
coming out, both the wrong sex,
and the wrong way around.
Not readily forgiven,

So you never nursed me
and when all my father's songs
couldn't sweeten the lack of money,
'when poverty comes through the door
love flies up the chimney',
your favourite saying,

Then you gave me away,
might never have known me,
if I had not cycled down
to court you like a young man,
teasingly untying your apron,
drinking by the fire, yarning

Of your wild, young days
which didn't last long, for you,
lovely Molly, the belle of your small town,
landed up mournful and chill
as the constant rain that lashes it
wound into your cocoon of pain.

Standing in that same hallway,
'Don't come again,' you say, roughly,
'I start to get fond of you, John,
and then you are up and gone';
the harsh logic of a forlorn woman
resigned to being alone.

And still, mysterious blessing,
I never knew, until you were gone,
that, always around your neck,
you wore an oval locket
with an old picture in it,
of a child in Brooklyn.

### I

The impulse in love
to name the place as
protection and solace;
an exact tenderness.
The way a room
can be so invested
with the presence
of a capable woman:
I see you bustling
around the house,
fragile and living,
tensely loving, as
long ago, my mother.
May she be granted,
*this houre, her Vigill,*
*a certain peace.*

### II

That we are here
for a time, that
we make our lives
carelessly, carefully,
as we are finally
also made by them;
a chosen companion,
a home, children;
on such conditions
I place my hopes
beside yours, Evelyn,
frail rope-ladders
across fuming oblivion.

### III

A new love, a new
litany of place names;
the hill city of Cork
lambent under rain,
the lamenting foghorn
at Roche's Point, hold-
ing its hoarse vigil
into a white Atlantic,
the shrouded shapes
of Mounts Brandon,
Sybil Head and Gabriel;
powers made manifest,
amulets against loneliness,
talismans for work:
a flowering presence?

BACK

*At the other end*
*of Ireland, a boat*
*is waiting, trestled*
*high above sand*
*and stone. A woman*
*is waiting, asleep*
*in a sunlit room —*
*our first haven —*
*above the Atlantic's*
*heaving lung.*

*In an adjoining room,*
*curled in her cot,*
*our first child draws*
*her honeyed breath;*
*a slighter rhythm.*
*One more death, and*
*the generation older*
*than Brendan and myself*
*will have gone to earth.*

*'To walk away, without*
*looking back, or crying':*
*an old Inuit saying,*
*simple folk wisdom.*
*The rites duly performed,*
*goodbyes decently said,*
*honour satisfied, we*
*head back across the*
*length of Ireland, home.*

2

Twice daily I carried water from the spring,
Morning before leaving for school, and evening;
Balanced as a fulcrum between two buckets.

A bramble-rough path ran to the river
 Where you stepped carefully across slime-topped stones,
With corners abraded as bleakly white as bones.

At the widening pool (for washing and cattle)
Minute fish flickered as you dipped,
Circling to fill, with rust-tinged water.

The second or enamel bucket was for spring water
Which, after racing through a rushy meadow,
Came bubbling in a broken drain-pipe,

Corroded wafer thin with rust.
It ran so pure and cold, it fell
Like manacles of ice on the wrists.

You stood until the bucket brimmed
Inhaling the musty smell of unpicked berries,
That heavy greenness fostered by water.

Recovering the scene, I had hoped to stylize it,
Like the portrait of an Egyptian water carrier:
But pause, entranced by slight but memoried life.

I sometimes come to take the water there,
Not as return or refuge, but some pure thing,
Some living source, half-imagined and half-real,

Pulses in the fictive water that I feel.

As a child I was frightened by her
Busy with her bowl of tea in a farmhouse chimney corner,
Wrapped in a cocoon of rags and shawls.
'The Lord have mercy on him,'
'*Go ndeanaidh Dia trocaire ar a anam.*'
She rocked and crooned,
A doll's head mouthing under stained rafters.

'The fairies of Ireland and the fairies of Scotland
Fought on that hill all night
And in the morning the well ran blood.
The dead queen was buried on that hill.
St Patrick passed by the mound:
There is the mark of a footprint forever
Where he stood to pray.'

Eyes rheumy with racial memory;
Fragments of bread soaked in brown tea
And eased between shrunken gums.
Her clothes stank like summer flax;
Watched all day as she swayed
Towards death between memories and prayers
By a farmer's child in a rough play-box.

'Mrs McGurren had the evil eye,
She prayed prayers on the black cow:
It dropped there and died,
Dropped dead in its tracks.
She stood on the mearing and cursed the Clarkes:
They never had a good day since,
Fluke and bad crops and a child born strange.'

In the groove a running-down record,
Heavy with local history:
Only the scratching now, the labouring breath,
Prophecy rattling aged bones.
Age is neither knowledge nor authority,
Though it may claim both,
Weaving a litany of legends against death.

But in high summer as the hills burned with corn
I strode through golden light
To the secret spirals of the burial stone:
The grass-choked well ran sluggish red —
Not with blood but ferrous rust —
But beneath the whorls of the guardian stone
What fairy queen lay dust?

SICK CALL

*for Seamus*

When the doctor disappeared
Under the thatched lintel
To tend a farmer who had
Fallen under his tractor
I tramped moodily back
And forwards in the snow

Meeting my own drowning
Footprints, as I turned,
Seeing, as the dog barked,
The trees, isolated and black
Against the grey, whirling
Bowl of the sky.

From the oblong of light
His wife called me over,
To relate, confidentially,
(The cur whining at her apron)
How hard it was, having
Her husband 'in a bad way'.

As my brother's car rocked
Down the rutted lane
Scattering a powder of snow,
The dog resumed its yelping,
Plunging at the wheels
And back to safety again.

In the girdered dark
of the byre, cattle move;
warm engines hushed
to a siding groove

before the switch flicks
down for milking.
In concrete partitions
they rattle their chains

while the farmhand eases
rubber tentacles to tug
lightly but rhythmically
on their swollen dugs

and up the pale cylinders
of the milking machine
mounts an untouched
steadily pulsing stream.

Only the tabby steals
to dip its radar whiskers
with old-fashioned relish
in a chipped saucer

and before Seán lurches
to kick his boots off
in the night-silent kitchen
he draws a mug of froth

to settle on the sideboard
under the hoard of delph.
A pounding transistor shakes
the Virgin on her shelf

as he dreams towards bed.
A last glance at a magazine,
he puts the mug to his head,
grunts, and drains it clean.

He wakes to a confused dream of boats, gulls,
And all his raw present floats
Suddenly up to him on rocking rails.
Through that long first day
He trudges streets, tracks friends,
Stares open-mouthed at monuments
To manufacturers, sabred generals.
Passing a vegetable stall
With exposed fruits, he halts
To contemplate a knobbly potato.

At lunchtime, in a cafeteria,
He finds his feet and hands
Enlarge, become like foreign lands.
A great city is darkness, noise
Through which bright girls move
Like burnished other children's toys.
Soon the whistling factory
Will lock him in:
Half-stirred memories and regrets
Drawn into that iron din.

*Tara, though she be desolate today,*
*Once was the habitation of heroes. . . .*
— from *The Book of Leinster*

I

The deep cooing of doves
As we move towards the earthen fort
Is a subtly insidious music
Designed to exhort:
Axehead of the intellect washed
In hovering fragrance of hawthorn,
The primary colours of a summer morning.

II

This martial extravagance of mounds
Cannot be approached simply:
Through ritual sagas it resounds
With din of war and love.
Devious virgins and fisty men
Gesturing against the sky,
Invoke the seasonal crucifixion.

III

Gaelic Acropolis or smoky hovel?
In the enormous osiered banquet hall
The sotted bards rehearse
A genealogical glory:
Stately assonance of verse
Petrifies wolf-skinned warriors
In galleries of race.

IV

Who longs for subtler singing,
Muted vocal of the dove,
Seeks erotic terror ringing
Over stony beds of love:
Couple and landscape blended,
Till beneath the hunchback mountain
Plunges the boar of death.

V

A battle of miracles
Proves the Christian dispensation,
Druidic snow turning
To merciful Christian rain:
Christ is the greater magician.
No more the phallic stone
Screams for its ritual king.

VI

A mournful St Patrick surveys
This provincial magnificence;
He sees what twitching sentries saw
When five regal roads
Across a landscape drew:
The central lands of Meath dissolve
Into royal planes of blue.

And now, at last, all proud deeds done,
Mouths dust-stopped, dark they embrace,
Suitably disposed, as urns, underground.
Cattle munching soft spring grass —
Epicures of shamrock and the four-leaved clover —
Hear a whimper of ancient weapons,
As a whole dormitory of heroes turn over,
Regretting their butchers' days.
This valley cradles their archaic madness
As once, on an impossibly epic morning,
It upheld their savage stride:
To bagpiped battle marching,
Wolfhounds, lean as models,
At their urgent heels.


SOLILOQUY ON A SOUTHERN STRAND

*A priest, holidaying on the coast outside Sydney,
thinks nostalgically of his boyhood in Ireland.*

When I was young, it was much simpler;
I saw God standing on a local hill,
His eyes were gentle and soft birds
Sang in chorus to his voice until
My body trembled, ardent in submission.
The friar came to preach the yearly sermon
For Retreat, and cried among the flaring candles:
'O children, children, if you but knew,
Each hair is counted, everything you do
Offends or sweetens His five wounds!'
A priest with a harsh and tuneless voice,
Raising his brown-robed arms to cry:
'Like this candle-end, the body gutters out to die!'
Calling us all to do penance and rejoice.

Hearing the preacher speak, I knew my mind
And wished to serve, leaving the friendly farm
For years of college. At first I found it strange
And feared the boys with smoother hands and voices:
I lay awake at night, longed for home.

I heard the town boys laughing in the dark
At things that made me burn with shame,
And where the votive candles whispered into wax
Hesitantly I spoke my treasured doubts,
Conquering all my passions in your Name.
I weathered years of strangeness
Until I stood before the Cathedral altar,
A burly country boy but new-made priest;
My mother watched in happiness and peace.

The young people crowd the shore now,
Rushing from Sydney, like lemmings, to the sea.
Heat plays upon the glaring cluttered beach,
Casts as in a mould my beaten head and knees.
New cars come swooping in like birds
To churn and chop the dust. A wireless,
Stuck in the sand, crackles love-sick static
As girls are roughed and raced
With whirling beach-balls in the sun.
What here avails my separate cloth,
My sober self, whose meaning contradicts
The sensual drama they enact in play?
'Hot Lips, Hot Lips', the throaty singer sighs:
A young man preens aloft and dives.

Is this the proper ending for a man?
The Pacific waves crash in upon the beach,
Roll and rise and inward stretch upon the beach.
It is December now and warm,
And yet my blood is cold, my shoulders slack;
In slow submission, I turn my body
Up to the sun, as on a rack,
Enduring comfort. In a dream,
I hear the cuckoo dance his double notes,
Among the harvest stooks like golden chessmen;
Each call, an age, a continent between.
No martyrdom, no wonder, no patent loss:
Is it for this mild ending that I
Have carried, all this way, my cross?

*California, 1956*

God watches from the cracked mirror on the wall.
God is a peeping-Tom, cat-like watches all.
When the stallion plunges, God is the rider,
With dark beard, back straight as a wall.
When I cut my hand or cheek in shaving
His blood flows and there is nothing at all
To protect me from the shadow of His redemption,
My godhead hung in text of terror on the wall.

As I pass in the street the young girls cry,
Lift their light skirts and cry,
And the blackbird mocks from the cherry tree,
Lifting its wings to cry:
'Shapeless, shapeless man in black,
What is that donkey's cross upon your back,
As the young girls lift their skirts and cry,
O! listless man in sunshine wearing black!'

It is Spring again, the trout feed,
The young sap stirs and flows like sluggish blood;
More people come to Mass and better dressed:
In the mountain I heard the sighing crack of guns
And the mirror in my hand cracked too
And ran in blood and my hands were blood
Until the burning sun came down and stood
Against my sky at three, in blood.

# 1

*Speech for an Ideal Irish Election*

Then the visionary lady
Walked like a magician's daughter
Across green acres of Ireland;
The broad bright sword
Of the politician's word
Summoned the applause in every square.

The unseen inhabited
A well, a corner of a field;
Houses assumed magic light
From patriots' memory;
Assemblies knelt in awe before
The supernatural in a shaking tree.

The light that never was
Enlarged profile, gun and phrase:
Green of the grass worn
On shoulder as catalytic token;
Acrid speech of rifle and gun
Easing neurosis into definite action.

The house subsides into stillness,
Buried bombs ignore the spade.
The evening light, suitably grave,
Challenges renewed activity.
The transfigured heroes assume
Grey proportions of statuary.

Now the extraordinary hour of calm
And day of limitation.
The soft grasses stir
Where unfinished dreams
Are buried with the Fianna
In that remote rock cave.

Who today asks for more —
Smoke of battle blown aside —
Than the struggle with casual
Graceless unheroic things,
The greater task of swimming
Against a slackening tide?


## 2

*Caledon Castle*

That was my first glimpse of opulence;
A line of peacocks deployed upon the lawn
Before a wide-windowed house.
And I was five and clutched a larger hand,
Marvelling how the marvellous birds
Expanded their wild tails like fans.
Under the warm trees, the deer grazed,
Under the walls, the peacocks strayed,
Under the windows, stone fountains played,
In a doomed and formal dance of opulence.


## 3

*Slum Clearance*

Standing at the window, I watch the wild green leaves
Lurch back against the wall, all the branches of the apple tree
Stretch tight before the wind, the rain lash
The evening long against the sullen buildings
Raised by man, the blackened rubbish dumps,
The half-built flats, the oozing grey cement
Of hasty walls, the white-faced children
Deprived of sun, scurrying with sharp laughter
From point to point of shelter,
And arched over all, the indifferent deadening rain.

# 4

*Emigrants*

Sad faced against the rails,
Suitcases clasped in awkward hands,
They throng the landing stage.
No one would think they go to quest
The shining Grail, the Great Good Place:
Incomprehension is heavy on every face.
Poor subjects for prose or verse,
In their grief, as animals, most piteous.

# 5

*Incantation in Time of Peace*

At times on this island, at the sheltered edge of Europe,
The last flowering garden of prayer and pretence,
Green enclosure of monks and quiet poetry,
Where the rivers move, without haste, to a restless sea,
And the rain shifts like a woven veil
Over headland and sleeping plain;
At times in this island, dreaming all day
In the sunlight and rain of attained revolutions,
We are afraid, as the hints pile up, of disaster,
Enlarged as a dinosaur, rising from the salt flats,
The webbed marshes of history, making the hand tremble,
Hardly knowing why.

At times, we watch the gradual progress of days
In this last casual fortress, separate by sea
And by choice from all men's fears and alarms,
All signs of shattered unity referred
To the benign and exclusive care of the Trinity,
Who today in our hour of need, seem indifferent and far
Over the shuttered and graceful hills,
In a more blessed land, where peace is the air,
And praise grazes in every fresh pasture;
There, our withdrawn ancestors, deserving of rest,
Kneel among dark rocks, in incessant
Contemplative prayer.

At times, we turn in most ordinary weakness and trembling
From the incense rising, the gentle light falling
On damp slum tenement and holy mountain;
From the safety of private quarrels, the candid forgiving,
Turn with hands eager in wishing
To assist all those fearful, exiled, and ailing,
Implicit in outstretched palms
Pulsing from the woven wrists like doves in flight
This need to be sharing,
And know against this backcloth
Our best longings helpless, as the clouds begin banking
For yet a more ominous day.

*1953*

WILD SPORTS OF THE WEST

The landlord's coat is tulip red,
A beacon on the wine-dark moor;
He turns his well-bred foreign devil's face,
While his bailiff trots before.

His furious hooves drum fire from stone,
A beautiful sight when gone;
Contemplation holds the noble horseman
In his high mould of bone.

Not so beautiful the bandy bailiff,
Churlish servant of an alien will:
Behind the hedge a maddened peasant
Poises his shotgun for the kill.

Evening brings the huntsman home,
Blood of pheasants in a bag:
Beside a turf-rick the cackling peasant
Cleanses his ancient weapon with a rag.

The fox, evicted from the thicket,
Evades with grace the snuffling hounds:
But a transplanted bailiff, in a feudal paradise,
Patrols for God His private grounds.

'God save our shadowed lands
Stalked by this night beast of the dead —
Turnip roundness of the skull,
Sockets smouldering in the head —
Will no St George or Patrick come,
Restore to us our once blessed
And blossoming, now barren, home?'

He paused on the threshold,
Clashed his sword of wood,
His swinging lantern on the snow
Threw blood-red circles where he stood;
Herded listeners gaped
Like goslings, as if they understood.

Bold as brass, a battering knight
Came roaring through the door,
Bussed the ladies on his right,
Smashed the devil to the floor.
Simple justice triumphs on the spot,
With straw, like guts, strewn everywhere:
False Satan struts no more.

A scene in farmhouse darkness,
Two wearing decades ago;
From which I best recall
Their faces like listening animals,
A stormlamp swinging to and fro,
And from those creaking rustic rhymes,
That purging lament of bad times.

Children learn the first lesson of fear in the night,
Hearing the clock talk as though to itself,
The lost birds crying under the creak of branches,
The *drip-drip* of a water-tap, and something moving
That could be alive, like a rat or a mouse,
But inhabits the dark without reason.

Islanded in the night, the young and the sleepless hear
The slight edge of the curtain twitching and shifting
And rubbing the dark, the murmur of walls
When dimensions are hidden, and suddenly fear
This absence of clear light, and the family of objects
That can be touched by a finger:

Golliwog with gross eyes dead in a corner,
Jack-in-the-Box who murdered Jack Horner,
Cinderella betrayed by the giant ogre,
Sinbad-the-Sailor with the great Roc on his back,
Stridently calling, and Tom the Piper's son,
Fleeing in fear from a grotesque father.

CULTURAL CENTRE: *MUSÉE IMAGINAIRE*

*Room 1*

The central crucifix from which the rigid figure
Hangs, minatory and Catalan;
The robust contours of an imperial brow,
Nose bridge spanned according to a law,
With lips that barely condescend to form a kiss
(Since Roman virtue is chief end on earth
And desire sufficient without spirit's rebirth);
While in a corner the Indian God
With multiplying hands, makes strange appeal
For concord, even in a place crowded
And wild with views as this:
His is a sort of benign and universal kiss.

*Room II*

Through corridors, in juxtaposed grace
Conflicting modes assume their permanence.
This lady has the pure Renaissance face
Of a Botticelli virgin in vernal radiance;
This tapestry has birds that lift their wings
In gestures of freedom from the woven silk.
How lightly the Japanese mountain rests its weight,
As though not intending to offend the earth!
And all this delicacy confronts, affronts,
The stark and staring crucifix.

*Room III*

Europe is dying, these motions say,
With this sharp body twisted all awry,
These diagrams in horror from a burnt-out city,
A canvas sprawling like a battlefield, with slaughtered forms,
While bright and clear, subduing all,
A complete abstraction judges us,
From its clean white wall.

*Entrance Hall*

A tiny nun is leading her whole class
Of chattering girls, through buildings
Perfectly constructed from pure glass,
To where this version of her vision stands:
At her corded waist swings
A minute harmless god of silver plate,
Until at last, inoffensive, starched and mild,
She stands possessively beneath
The lean, accusing, Catalan crucifix.

*New Haven, 1954*

## BUS STOP, NEVADA

The blind, the halt, the lame descend these steps.
This cheapest form of transport gets its trade
From God's worst handiwork, the botched and poorly paid
In a land of honey. The anaemic lady,
The heavy shop-girl rush into desert sunlight,
Blazing a trail with comic books and smoke
To where, in a sullen cafeteria,
Coffee-engines snort and cheap pies line the glass.
Hands ply the glossy cranks of slot-machines,
Dreaming catharsis through a deluge of coins.
Beyond, the snow-capped Sierras bluntly rise:
Suggest, even in high summer, skiers' curving ease.
Travellers raise their bored and famished eyes
To where snow and forest limn the weightless skies.

## IRISH STREET SCENE, WITH LOVERS

A rainy quiet evening, with leaves that hang
Like squares of silk from dripping branches.
An avenue of laurel, and the guttering cry
Of a robin that balances a moment,
Starts and is gone
Upon some furtive errand of its own.

A quiet evening, with skies washed and grey;
A tiredness as though the day
Swayed towards sleep,
Except for the reserved statement
Of rain on the stone-grey pavement —
Dripping, they move through this marine light,

Seeming to swim more than walk,
Linked under the black arch of an umbrella
With its assembly of spokes like points of stars,
A globule of water slowly forming on each.
The world shrinks to the soaked, worn
Shield of cloth they parade beneath.

WOODTOWN MANOR

*for Morris Graves*

I

Here the delicate dance of silence,
The quick step of the robin,
The sudden skittering rush of the wren:
Minute essences move in and out of creation
Until the skin of soundlessness forms again.

Part order, part wilderness,
Water creates its cadenced illusion
Of glaucous, fluent growth;
Fins raised, as in a waking dream,
Bright fish probe their painted stream.

Imaginary animals harbour here:
The young fox coiled in its covert,
Bright-eyed and mean, the baby bird:
The heron, like a radiant italic,
Illuminating the gospel of the absurd.

And all the menagerie of the living marvellous:
Stone shape of toad,
Flicker of insect life,
Shift of wind-touched grass
As though a beneficent spirit stirred.

II

Twin deities hover in Irish air
Reconciling poles of east and west;
The detached and sensual Indian God,
Franciscan dream of gentleness:
Gravity of Georgian manor
Approves, with classic stare,
Their dual disciplines of tenderness.

TIM

Not those slim-flanked fillies
slender-ankled as models
glimpsed across the rails
through sunlong afternoons
as with fluent fetlocks
they devoured the miles

Nor at some Spring Show
a concourse of Clydesdales
waiting, huge as mammoths,
as enormous hirsute dolls,
for an incongruous rose to
blossom behind their ears

Nor that legendary Pegasus
leaping towards heaven:
only those hold my affection
who, stolid as weights,
rested in the rushy
meadows of my childhood

Or rumbled down lanes,
lumbering before carts.
Tim, the first horse I rode,
seasick on his barrel
back; the first to lip
bread from my hand.

I saw the end of your road.
You stood, with gouged eyeball
while our farmhand swabbed
the hurt socket out with
water and Jeyes Fluid:
as warm an object of

loving memory, as any
who have followed me
to this day, denying
rhetoric with your patience,
forcing me to drink
from the trough of reality.

*According to* Leabhar Gabhála, *The Book of Conquests, the first invasion of Ireland was by relatives of Noah, just before the Flood. Refused entry into the Ark, they consulted an idol which told them to flee to Ireland. There were three men and fifty-one women in the party.*

Fleeing from threatened flood, they sailed,
Seeking the fair island, without serpent or claw;
From the deck of their hasty raft watched
The soft edge of Ireland nearward draw.

A sweet confluence of waters, a trinity of rivers,
Was their first resting place:
They unloaded the women and the sensual idol,
Guiding image of their disgrace.

Division of damsels they did there,
The slender, the tender, the dimpled, the round,
It was the first just bargain in Ireland,
There was enough to go round.

Lightly they lay and pleasured
In the green grass of that guileless place:
Ladhra was the first to die;
He perished of an embrace.

Bith was buried in a stone heap,
Riot of mind, all passion spent.
Fintan fled from the ferocious women
Lest he, too, by love be rent.

Great primitive princes of our line —
They were the first, with stately freedom,
To sleep with women in Ireland:
Soft the eternal bed they lie upon.

On a lonely headland the women assembled,
Chill as worshippers in a nave,
And watched the eastern waters gather
Into a great virile flooding wave.

# ALL LEGENDARY OBSTACLES

IN DEDICATION

My love, while we talked
They removed the roof. Then
They started on the walls,
Panes of glass uprooting
From timber, like teeth.
But you spoke calmly on,
Your example of courtesy
Compelling me to reply.
When we reached the last
Syllable, nearly accepting
Our positions, I saw that
The floorboards were gone:
It was clay we stood upon.

# 1

OBSESSION

Once again, the naked girl
Dances on the lawn
Under the horrible trees
Smelling of rain
And ringed Saturn leans
His vast ear over the world:

But though everywhere the unseen
(Scurry of feet, scrape of flint)
Are gathering, I cannot
Protest. My tongue
Lies curled in my mouth —
My power of speech is gone.

Thrash of an axle in snow!
Not until the adept faun-
Headed brother approves
Us both from the darkness
Can my functions return.
*Like clockwork, I strike and go.*

# 2

THE TROUT

*for Barrie Cooke*

Flat on the bank I parted
Rushes to ease my hands
In the water without a ripple
And tilt them slowly downstream
To where he lay, tendril-light,
In his fluid sensual dream.

Bodiless lord of creation,
I hung briefly above him
Savouring my own absence,
Senses expanding in the slow
Motion, the photographic calm
That grows before action.

As the curve of my hands
Swung under his body
He surged, with visible pleasure.
I was so preternaturally close
I could count every stipple
But still cast no shadow, until

The two palms crossed in a cage
Under the lightly pulsing gills.
Then (entering my own enlarged
Shape, which rode on the water)
I gripped. To this day I can
Taste his terror on my hands.

# 3

COUNTRY MATTERS

I

They talk of rural innocence but most marriages
Here (or wherever the great middle-
Class morality does not prevail) are arranged
*Post factum,* products of a warm night,
A scuffle in a ditch, boredom spiced
By curiosity, by casual desire —
That ancient game. . . .
                   Rarely
  That ancient sweetness.

                   In school
Her hair was unstinted as harvest
Inundating her thin shoulderblades
Almost to her waist. As she ran
The boys called and raced after her
Across the schoolyard, repeating her name
Like something they meant. Until she stopped:
Then they dwindled away, in flight
From a silence.

            But after dark
The farmhands came flocking to her door
Like vagrant starlings, to sit by the fireside
Pretending indifference, or hang around outside
Waiting for a chance to call her away
Down the slope, into darkness.

                Finally,
Of course, she gave in. Flattered,
Lacking shrewdness, lacking a language?

## II

By the time she was fourteen she was known
As a 'good thing'. By the time she was sixteen
She had to go to England 'to get rid of it'.
By the time she was eighteen, no one 'decent'
Or 'self-respecting' would touch her:
With her tangle of hair and nervously
Darkened eyes, she looked and spoke like
'A backstreets whure'.
                              Condemnation
Never lacks a language!

## III

She married, eventually, some casual
Labourer from the same class as herself
For in the countryside even beauty
Cannot climb stairs. But my eye
Still follows an early vision when
Grace inhabited her slight form;
Though my hesitant need to praise
Has had to wait a sanction
Greater than sour morality's
To see the light of day:
                              For lack of courage
                              Often equals lack of a language
                              And the word of love is
                              Hardest to say.

# 4

VIRGO HIBERNICA

Dare I yet confront
that memory? She poses
on a moist hillside or
stalks through the groin
of the woods on Sunday
mornings, an innocently
accomplished huntress,
acorns snapping beneath
         her feet.

Her hair is chestnut
light over the stained
freedom of a raincoat;
each breast kernel-slight
under unbleached wool:
as I trudge docile
by her flank, I feel
the gravitational pull
         of love.

And fight back, knowing
gold of her cheekbones,
her honeyed, naïve speech
drains power from manhood;
yet for years we walk
Enniskerry, Sallygap,
clasped in talk, neither
willing to let the other
         come or go . . .

# 5

ALL LEGENDARY OBSTACLES

All legendary obstacles lay between
Us, the long imaginary plain,
The monstrous ruck of mountains
And, swinging across the night,
Flooding the Sacramento, San Joaquin,
The hissing drift of winter rain.

All day I waited, shifting
Nervously from station to bar
As I saw another train sail
By, the San Francisco Chief or
Golden Gate, water dripping
From great flanged wheels.

At midnight you came, pale
Above the negro porter's lamp.
I was too blind with rain
And doubt to speak, but
Reached from the platform
Until our chilled hands met.

You had been travelling for days
With an old lady, who marked
A neat circle on the glass
With her glove, to watch us
Move into the wet darkness
Kissing, still unable to speak.

# 6

SENTENCE FOR KONARAK

Extravagantly your stone gestures
encourage and ease our desires
till the clamour dies: it is not
that man is a bare forked animal,
but that sensuousness is betrayed
by sensuality (a smell of burning flesh);

though here face turns to face,
not ashamed (the word barely exists,
so calm the movement, limpid the smile
above your monstrous actions)
that we are rebuked to learn
how, in the proper atmosphere,

the stealthy five-fingered hand
is less thief than messenger,
as the god bends towards her
whose head already sways towards him,
pliant as a lily, while round them,
in a teeming richness, move

the ripe-thighed temple dancers
in a field of force, a coiling honeycomb
of forms, the golden wheel of love.

# 7

LOVING REFLECTIONS

I *Amo, ergo sum*

I hold your ashen
Face in the hollow
Of my hand and warm
It slowly back to life.
As the eyelashes stir
Exposing brown, flecked
Pupils, soft with
Belief in my existence,
I make a transference
Of trust, and know
The power of the magician:
My palm begins to glow.

II *The Blow*

Anger subsiding, I could
Still see the fiery mark
Of my fingers dwindle
On your cheek, but
Did not rush to kiss
The spot. Hypocrisy
Is not love's agent,
Though our fierce awareness
Would distort instinct
To stage a mood.

III *Pitch-Dark*

Truths we upturn
Too near the bone;
Shudder of angels
Into grimacing stone:
Whatever hope we
Woke with, gone.
We cannot imagine
A further dawn.
Only the will says —
*Soldier on!*

# 8

THAT ROOM

Side by side on the narrow bed
We lay, like chained giants,
Tasting each other's tears, in terror
Of the news which left little to hide
But our two faces that stared
To ritual masks, absurd and flayed.

Rarely in a lifetime comes such news
Shafting knowledge straight to the heart
Making shameless sorrow start —
Not childish tears, querulously vain —
But adult tears that hurt and harm,
Seeping like acid to the bone.

Sound of hooves on the midnight road
Raised a romantic image to mind:
The Dean riding late to Marley?
But we must suffer the facts of self;
No one endures another's fate
And no one will ever know

What happened in that room
But when we came to leave
We scrubbed each other's tears,
Prepared the usual show. That day
Love's claims made chains of time and place
To bind us together more: equal in adversity.

# 9

THE WATER'S EDGE

Two of your landscapes I take:
The long loneliness of *Berck-Plage*
Where you walked, in your plaid uniform,
Directly into the wind.

Or the formal procession
Of horses, under the trim oaks
Of that urban forest where
You first learnt to ride.

There is in love that brief
Jealousy of the other's past
Coming on the charred roots
Of feeling, of ancient grief;

And here, in a third place,
Two of your landscapes seem to join
In a sweet conspiracy of mirrored
Surfaces, to baffle time

As the now heraldic animal
Stands by the water's edge
Lifting its rider against the sky,
A human shield.

# 10

A CHARM

When you step near
I feel the dark hood
Descend, a shadow
Upon my mind.

One thing to do,
Describe a circle
Around, about me,
Over, against you:

The hood is still there
But my pupils burn
Through the harsh folds.
You may return

Only as I wish.
But how my talons
Ache for the knob
Of your wrist!

# 11

THE GRUAGACH

Simple herdsmen, lost in that valley,
Saw the brute-thighed giantess;
A sleight of shadow to dominate
Their minds. 'A gleam of sun
Across the mist threw monstrous images
Of our dirty and misshapen selves
Against the sky.'

        Thus the guide:
But some may still submit to giant
Lacerations of light, the mind
Scrabbling for hold, and wait
Until the mist slides to expose
A motionless curve of mountain,
Bleached ribs of rock.

## 12

A PRIVATE REASON

As I walked out at Merval with my wife
Both of us sad, for a private reason,
We found the perfect silence for it,
A beech leaf severed, like the last
Living thing in the world, to crease
The terraced snow, as we
Walked out by Merval.

And the long staged melancholy of *allées,*
Tree succeeding tree, each glazed trunk
Not a single heaven-invoking nakedness
But a clause, a cold commentary
Of branches, gathering to the stripped
Dignity of a sentence, as we
Walked out by Merval.

There is a sad formality in the Gallic dance,
Linking a clumsy calligraphy of footsteps
With imagined princes, absorbing sorrow
In a larger ritual, a lengthening avenue
Of perspectives, the ice-gripped pond
Our only Hall of Mirrors, as we
Walk back from Merval.

# 13

RETURN

From the bedroom you can see
straight to the fringe of the woods
with a cross staved gate to re-
enter childhood's world:
                              the pines
wait, dripping.


                    Crumbling black-
berries, seized from a rack
of rusty leaves, maroon tents
of mushroom, pillars uprooting
with a dusty snap;


                    as the bucket
fills, a bird strikes from the bushes
and the cleats of your rubber boot crush
a yellow snail's shell to a smear
on the grass
                    (while the wind starts
the carrion smell of the dead fox
staked as warning).


                    Seeing your former
self saunter up the garden path
afterwards, would you flinch,
acknowledging
                    that sensuality,
that innocence?

*for John McGahern*

At times I see it, present
    As a bright day, or a hill,
The only way of saying something
    Luminously as possible.

Not the accumulated richness
    Of an old historical language —
That musk-deep odour!
    But a slow exactness

Which recreates experience
    By ritualizing its details —
Pale web of curtain, width
    Of deal table, till all

Takes on a witch-bright glow
    And even the clock on the mantel
Moves its hands in a fierce delight
    Of so, and so, and so.

By the crumbling fire we talked
Animal-dazed by the heat
While the lawyer unhooked a lamp
From peat blackened rafters
And climbed the circle of stairs.

Without, the cattle, heavy for milking,
Shuddered and breathed in the byre.
'It falls early these nights,' I said
Lifting tongs to bruise a turf
And hide the sound of argument upstairs

From an old man, hands clenched
On rosary beads, and a hawthorn stick
For hammering the floor —
A nuisance in the working daytime,
But now, signing a parchment,

Suddenly important again, as long before.
Cannily aware of his final scene too,
With bald head swinging like a stone
In irresistible statement: 'It's rightly theirs.'
Or: 'They'll never see stick of mine.'

Down in the kitchen, husband and wife
Watched white ash form on the hearth,
Nervously sharing my cigarettes,
While the child wailed in the pram
And a slow dark overcame fields and farm.

All that bone-bright winter's day
He completed my angle of sight
Patterning the hill field
With snaky furrows,
The tractor chimney smoking
Like his pipe, under the felt hat.

Ten years ago, it was a team
With bulky harness and sucking step
That changed our hill:
Grasping the cold metal
The tremble of the earth
Seemed to flow into one's hands.

Still the dark birds shape
Away as he approaches
To sink with a hovering
Fury of open beaks —
Starling, magpie, crow ride
A gunmetal sheen of gaping earth.

Jimmy Drummond used bad language at school,
All the four-letter words, like a drip from a drain.
At six he knew how little children were born,
As well he might, since his mother bore nine,
Six after her soldier husband left for the wars

Under the motto of the Royal Irish, *Clear the Way!*
When his body returned from England
The authorities told them not to unscrew the lid
To see the remnants of Fusilier Drummond inside —
A chancey hand-grenade had left nothing to hide

And Jimmy's mother was pregnant at the graveside —
Clear the way, and nothing to hide.
Love came to her punctually each springtime,
Settled in the ditch under some labouring man:
'It comes over you, you have to lie down.'

Her only revenge on her hasty lovers
Was to call each child after its father,
Which the locals admired, and seeing her saunter
To collect the pension of her soldier husband
Trailed by her army of baby Irregulars.

Some of whom made soldiers for foreign wars,
Some supplied factories in England.
Jimmy Drummond was the eldest but died younger than an
When he fell from a scaffolding in Coventry
Condemned, like all his family, to *Clear the Way!*

## FORGE

The whole shed smelt of dead iron:
the dented teeth of a harrow,
the feminine pathos of donkeys' shoes.

A labourer backed in a Clydesdale.
Hugely fretful, its nostrils dilated
while the smith viced a hoof

in his apron, wrestling it
to calmness, as he sheared the pith
like wood-chips, to a rough circle.

Then the bellows sang in the tall chimney
waking the sleeping metal, to leap
on the anvil. As I was slowly

beaten to a matching curve
the walls echoed the stress
of the verb *to forge.*

## TIME OUT

The donkey sat down on the roadside
Suddenly, as though tired of carrying
His cross. There was a varnish
Of sweat on his coat, and a fly
On his left ear. The tinker
Beating him finally gave in,
Sat on the grass himself, prying
His coat for his pipe. The donkey
(Not beautiful but more fragile
Than any swan, with his small
Front hooves folded under him)
Gathered enough courage to raise
That fearsome head, lipping a daisy,
As if to say — slowly, contentedly —
Yes, there is a virtue in movement,
But only going so far, so fast,
Sucking the sweet grass of stubbornness.

# 1

*11 rue Daguerre*

At night, sometimes, when I cannot sleep
I go to the *atelier* door
And smell the earth of the garden.

It exhales softly,
Especially now, approaching springtime,
When tendrils of green are plaited

Across the humus, desperately frail
In their passage against
The dark, unredeemed parcels of earth.

There is white light on the cobblestones
And in the apartment house opposite —
All four floors — silence.

In that stillness — soft but luminously exact,
A chosen light — I notice that
The tips of the lately grafted cherry-tree

Are a firm and lacquered black.

# 2

*Salute, in passing, for Sam*

The voyagers we cannot follow
Are the most haunting. That face
Time has worn to a fastidious mask
Chides me, as one strict master
Steps through the Luxembourg.
Surrounded by children, lovers,
His thoughts are rigorous as trees
Reduced by winter. While the water
Parts for tiny white-rigged yachts
He plots an icy human mathematics —
Proving what content sighs when all
Is lost, what wit flares from nothingness:
His handsome hawk head is sacrificial
As he weathers to how man now is.

# 3

*Radiometers in the rue Jacob*

In the twin
Or triple crystalline spheres
The tiny fans of mica flash;
Snow fleeing on dark ground.

I imagine
One on an executive's desk
Whirling above the memoranda
Or by his mistress's bed

(Next to the milk-white telephone)

A minute wind-
Mill casting its pale light
Over unhappiness, ceaselessly
Elaborating its signals

Not of help, but of neutral energy.

# 1

*Enclosure*

Through the poplars we spy the broken
Shape of the château. No one wishes
To visit now, although sections
Of family stay through the summer,
Children chasing, gathering serrated
Pine-cones. Around the landscaped woods
The high stone wall no longer defines
But falters.

   As at twilight
Under the portraits of the long
Gallery (the ambassador to Russia,
The high-booted elegance of Turenne's
Aide-de-camp) the adults assemble
To the light ritual of a conversation
Determined before they were born.
Close to *Le Figaro* on the inlaid
Table rests *l'Almanach du Gotha,*
A closed book for a closed, and
Closing world.

    Though the window
Still frames the steeple, frail
As a lady's finger, of the family
Church where they were baptized
And married, with the school built
By their father, for the peasants' good
And the Mayor's house where, till lately,
He was master. A pattern of use
Dwindles to aesthetic views

                    Except
In this last room where blue Sèvres,
A bare-breasted Maenad, and dull
Gold of panelled walls preserve
The restraints of a style, over which
The massive teardrops of the chandelier
Suspend, shifting soundlessly,
Like a mobile.

# 2

*The Centenarian*

All afternoon we assemble, a cluster
of children, grand-children, great-
grand-children, in-laws like myself
come to celebrate this scant haired
talkative old lady's
long delaying action against death.

While technicians scurry to arrange
cables, and test for sound,
calmly on the lawn we dispose
ourselves; spokes of a wheel
radiating from that strict centre
where she holds her ground.

Skull cap like a Rembrandt Jew,
jowls weathered past yellow to old gold,
the hands in her lap discreetly folded
shelter a black morocco purse
containing (so the awed family claim)
a sound portfolio from the Paris *bourse*.

As the cameras whir she recites
her life, with the frightening babble
of the age liberated, entirely free:
how she knew the young Hussard captain
loved her, as passing her window
every morning, he lifted his *képi*:

how she drove through French and enemy lines
to recover her handsome cavalier son
buried in No Man's Land;
but the hasty planks of her home-
made coffin were too short:
his boot came away in her hand.

She does not raise her failing eyes
to heaven, to attest what she has undergone,
but treats Him like a gentleman
who will know how things are done
when she is finally gathered upwards
with, but not like, everyone. . . .

On the frost-held
field, Orpheus
strides, his greaves
bleak with light,
the split lyre
silver hard
in his hands;
sleek after him
the damp-tongued
cringing hounds.

An unaccountable
desire to kneel,
to pray, pulls
my hands but
his head is not
a crown of thorns:
a great antlered
stag, pity
shrinks from
those horns.

Your body is small,
squat, deformed as
a Nahuatl Indian,
an Aztec image
of necessary death:

casually born
of the swirl of
a river, tossed
up by tides —
sexual flotsam —

regard those swart
small breasts that
will never give milk
though around inflamed
nipples, love-bites

multiply like scars.
Salt wind of desire
upon the flesh!
Black hair swings
over your shoulders

as you bear darkness
down toward me, and
across the sun-robed
pyramid, obsidian knives
resume their sacrifice.

*I. M. Theodore Roethke*

I

There is no hawk among my friends.
Swiftly they cruise their chosen air,
Not to spy the grey fieldmouse
And plummet fiercely to the moor,
But to survey a heaven, inspect
The small, the far. Is it news
That the beetle's back is abstract,
A jewel box; the ash pod has glider wings?
Cruelty is not their way of life,
Nor indifference; they ride the currents
To grasp the invisible. The service
They do shapes also what they are
And the fernlike talon uncurls:
There is no hawk among my friends.

II

There are days when the head is
A bitter, predatory thing
Which will not let oneself
Or others alone, prying, rending!

It is a chill sensuality
Which outdistances cruelty
As though destruction were
A releasing element

Down which the mind patrols —
A wide vanned golden eagle —
Seizing the unnecessary, the small,
With juridical claws.

But sometimes when it sails
Too swift, between the wings' pause,
I know that my own best life
Is the hypnotized fieldmouse

Housed beneath its claws.

SWEETNESS

*I. M. Flann O'Brien, who skipped it*

So Sweeney flew on until he reached the church of Swim-Two-Birds
opposite Clonmacnois. He landed on a Friday, to be exact; the cler-
ics were chanting Nones while women beat flax and one was giving
birth. As he watched from his tree, Sweeney heard the Vesper bell
ring and felt compelled to this poem:

Although my claws weaken
Sweeter across water
The cuckoo's soft call
Than girn of church-bell.

Woman, don't give birth,
Nevertheless, on a Friday,
When even Mad Sweeney
Fasts for the King of Truth.

As the women scutch flax —
Though I say it myself —
So were my folk scutched
At the battle of Mag Rath.

From Loch Diolar of the cliffs
To Derry Colm Cille
It wasn't war I heard
From melodious, proud swans.

And the belling of the stag
In Siodhmhuine's steep glen;
No music on earth soothes
My soul like its sweetness.

O hear me, Christ
Without stain, never
Let me be severed,
Oh Christ, from your sweetness!

*from the Irish*

238

*for Robert Duncan*

Sean the hunchback, sadly
Walking the road at evening
Hears an errant music,
Clear, strange, beautiful,

And thrusts his moon face
Over the wet hedge
To spy a ring of noble
Figures dancing, with —

A rose at the centre —
The lustrous princess.

Humbly he pleads to join,
Saying, 'Pardon my ugliness,
Reward my patience,
Heavenly governess.'

Presto! Like the frog prince
His hump grows feather
Light, his back splits,
And he steps forth, shining

Into the world of ideal
Movement where (stripped
Of stale selfishness,
Curdled envy) all

Act not as they are
But might wish to be —
Planets assumed in
A sidereal harmony —

Strawfoot Sean
Limber as any.

But slowly old habits
Reassert themselves, he
Quarrels with pure gift,
Declares the boredom

Of a perfect music
And, with goatish nastiness,
Seeks first to insult,
Then rape, the elegant princess.

Presto! With a sound
Like a rusty tearing
He finds himself lifted
Again through the air

To land, sprawling,
Outside the hedge,
His satchel hump securely
Back on his back.

*Sean the hunchback, sadly*
*Walking the road at evening . . .*

PREMONITION

I

The darkness comes slowly alight.
That flow of red hair I recognise
Over the knob of the shoulder
Down your pale, freckled skin,
The breasts I have never seen;
But slowly the line of the tresses
Begins to stir, with a movement

That is not hair, but blood
Flowing. Someone is cutting
Your naked body up:
Strapped in dream helplessness
I hear each thrust of the knife
Till that rising, descending blade
Seems the final meaning of life.

Mutely, you writhe and turn
In tremors of ghostly pain,
But I am lost to intervene,
Blood, like a scarlet curtain,
Swinging across the brain
Till the light switches off —
And silence is darkness again.

II

On the butcher's block
Of the operating theatre
You open your eyes.
Far away, I fall back
Towards sleep, the Liffey
Begins to rise, and knock
Against the quay walls.

The gulls curve and scream
Over the Four Courts, over
This ancient creaking house
Where, released from dream,
I lie in a narrow room;
Low-ceilinged as a coffin
The dawn prises open.

# 1

*A Door Banging*

Downstairs, a door
banging, like a
blow upon sleep,

pain bleeding
away in gouts
of accusation &

counter accusation:
heart's release
of bitter speech.

# 2

*Mosquito Hunt*

Heat contracts the
walls, smeared with
the bodies of insects

we crush, absurd-
ly balanced on the
springs of the bed

twin shadows on
the wall rising
& falling as

we swoop &
quarrel, like
wide-winged bats.

# 3

*Tides*

The window blown
open, that summer
night, a full moon

occupying the sky
with a pressure of
underwater light,

a pale radiance
glossing the titles
behind your head

& the rectangle
of the bed where,
after long separation,

we begin to make
love quietly, bodies
turning like fish

in obedience to
the pull & tug
of your great tides.

In the Stadsmuzeum at Bruges, there is a picture by Gerard David of a man being flayed. Four craftsmen are concerned with the figure on the table: one is opening the left arm, another lifting away the right nipple, a third incising the right arm while the last (his knife caught between his teeth) is unwinding the results of his labour so as to display the rich network of veins under the skin of the left leg. The only expression in the faces of those looking on is a mild admiration: the Burgomeister has caught up the white folds of his ermine gown and is gazing into the middle distance. It is difficult even to say that there is any expression on the face of the victim, although his teeth are gritted and the cords attaching his wrist to the legs of the table are stretched tight. The whole scene may be intended as an allegory of human suffering but what the line of perspective leads us to admire is the brown calfskin of the principal executioner's boots.

MEDUSA

Again she appears,
The putrid fleshed woman
Whose breath is ashes,
Hair a writhing net of snakes!
Her presence strikes gashes
Of light into the skull,
Rears the genitals,

Tears away all
I had so carefully built —
Position, marriage, fame —
As heavily she glides towards me
Rehearsing the letters of my name
As if tracing them from
A rain streaked stone.

All night we turn
Towards an unsounded rhythm
Deeper, more fluent than breathing.
In the grey light of morning
Her body relaxes: the hiss of seed
Into that mawlike womb
Is the whimper of death being born.

SPECIAL DELIVERY

The spider's web
of your handwriting
on a blue envelope

brings up too much
to bear, old sea-sick-
ness of love, retch

of sentiment, night
& day devoured by
the worm of delight

which turns to
feed upon itself;
emotion running so

wildly to seed
between us that
it assumes a third,

a ghost or child's
face, the soft skull
frail as an eggshell

& the life-cord
of the emerging body —
fish, reptile, bird —

which trails
like the cable
of an astronaut

as we whirl & turn
in our bubble of
blood & sperm

before the gravities
of earth claim us
from limitless space.

Now, light-years later,
your nostalgic letter
admitting failure,

claiming forgiveness.
When fire pales to
so faint an ash,

so frail a design,
why measure guilt,
your fault or mine:

but blood seeps where
I sign before tearing
down the perforated line.

The infinite softness
& complexity of a body
in repose. The hinge

of the ankle bone de-
fines the flat space
of a foot, its puckered

flesh & almost arch.
The calf's heavy curve
sweeping down against

the bony shin, or up
to the warm bulges and
hollows of the knee

describes a line of
gravity, energy as
from shoulder knob

to knuckle, the arm
cascades, round the
elbow, over the wrist.

The whole body a system
of checks & balances —
those natural shapes

a sculptor celebrates,
sea-worn caves, pools,
boulders, tree-trunks —

              or, at every hand's turn,
              a crop of temptation:
              arm & thigh opening

on softer, more secret
areas, hair sprouting
crevices, odorous nooks

& crannies of love,
awaiting the impress
of desire, a fervent

homage, or tempting
to an extinction of
burrowing blindness.

(Deviously uncurling
from the hot clothes
of shame, a desert

father's dream of
sluttish nakedness,
demon with inflamed

breasts, dangling
tresses to drag man
down to hell's gaping

vaginal mouth.)

    To see the model
    as simply human

    a mild housewife
    earning pocket money .
    for husband, child,

    is to feel the dark
    centuries peel away
    to the innocence of

    the white track on
    her shoulders where
    above brown flesh

the brassiere lifts
to show the quiet of
unsunned breasts &

to mourn & cherish
each melancholy proof
of mortality's grudge

against perfection:
the appendix scar
lacing the stomach

the pale stitches on
the wailing wall of
the rib-cage where

the heart obediently
pumps.

What homage
is worthy for such

a gentle unveiling?
To nibble her ten
toes, in an ecstasy

of love, to drink
hair, like water?
(Fashion designers

would flatten her
breasts, level the
curves of arse &

stomach, moulding
the mother lode
that pulses beneath

to a uniformity
of robot bliss.)

On cartridge paper

an army of pencils
deploy silently to
lure her into their

net of lines while
from & above her
chilled, cramped

body blossoms
a late flower:
her tired smile.


## THE NORTHERN GATE

An owl hooted softly
but when I tried to follow
flitted from tree to tree —
the city turned forest —
as though to mock me.
By the Northern Gate
I thought I had located
him, and stood staring,
a dark head, searching
for a darker, through
darkness. Blunt wings
puffed for flight,
horny beak and white
flecked face: imagination
was firing so fast that
I built a feathered ghost
(down to the scaly talons
ringing the bark) from
a few swaying branches
and then turned to hear
him clearing his throat
somewhere behind me, as
if for a parting note —
but a sigh of airbrakes
from a morning lorry
drowned him out.

TO CEASE

*for Samuel Beckettt*

> *To cease*
> *to be human.*
>
> To be
> a rock down
> which rain pours,
> a granite jaw
> slowly discoloured.
>
> Or a statue
> sporting a giant's beard
> of verdigris or rust
> in some forgotten
> village square.
>
> A tree worn
> by the prevailing winds
> to a diagram of
> tangled branches:
> gnarled, sapless, alone.
>
> To cease
> to be human
> and let birds soil
> your skull, animals rest
> in the crook of your arm.
>
> To become
> an object, honoured
> or not, as the occasion demands;
> while time bends you slowly
> back to the ground.

Under the dented hat
with high black band;

that long face, sloping
like a gable down
to the jutting jaw;
sallow skin, scant
moustache, swallowed

by dark sudden-
ly glinting glasses

those slender fingers
cramped around a
walking stick or
white wine glass;
it could be my

father or yours;
any worn, life-

tempered man if
the caption lacked
the detail — bright as
heresiarch or fallen
angel — of his name.

## SEA CHANGES

## 1

*Each rock pool a garden*
*Of colour, bronze and*
*Blue gleam of Irish moss,*
*Rose of coral algae,*
*Ochre of sponge where*
*Whelk and starfish turn*
*In an odour of low tide;*
*Faint odour of stillness.*

# 2

*Net*

Splash! and a rusty cordage
of shapes descends through levels
of water.
         They could be mistaken
for seaweed, so cloudily they uncoil
and tumble
           so little they displace
in this mobile world, as obediently
they settle
        where blind, fluent
shoals, a ghostly tremor of wills,
seek their path;
            skirting rocks,
cold gush of currents, swerving up,
aside, like wraiths:
           red-faced gurnard,
slate-blue mackerel, sleek, leathery eel
of the Bermoothes —
             (are we ourselves, or
the air we breathe? Half-hidden motives,
knot of purposes) —
          pale flaps of gills
open and fold, mute mouths knead, till
like quicksilver
         keen to danger, dissolve
and shoot against the roof of their world,
all flickering instinct
          that will be cut
short as the lattice of ropes intercepts
and tightens;
        a tourniquet of death!

# 3

*Undertow*

Nothing is ever still.
Descend into the harsh
Emerald of the sea-depths.
Frond and mollusc,
Coral and seahorse,
Surely this balletic lull
Is the final nursery
Of sway in silence
Where fish break the
Glass of an element
As by magic.

          But
      Nothing is ever still.
      The crab's metallic arm
      Creaks from the stone,
      The transparent shrimp
      Scuttles beneath rain-
      Bow shoals, fleeing before
      The curving predators,
      Part of the slow, perpetual
      Fall of small things
      Down to the rising
      Aggregate of the seabed.

            Die or devour! But
            Everything dies into birth.
            On the clambering vacuum
            Of the sea floor, something
            Grows, begins to spread,
            A ceaseless, blind
            Flickering, rain
            Turning to snow
            Drifting to sleet,
            A veil of movement
            That accumulates, melts
            Into one relentlessly
            Converging lathe of power-
            ful motion: the menace
            of the undertow!

# 4

*Wine Dark Sea*

For there is no sea
it is all a dream
there is no sea
except in the tangle
of our minds:
the wine dark
sea of history
on which we all turn
turn and thresh
     and disappear.

# A SLOW DANCE

**1**

SWEENEY

A wet silence.
Wait under trees,
muscles tense,
ear lifted, eye alert.

Lungs clear.
A nest of senses
stirring awake —
*human beast!*

A bird lights:
two claw prints.
Two leaves shift:
a small wind.

Beneath, white
rush of current,
stone chattering
between high banks.

Occasional shrill
of a bird, squirrel
trampolining along
a springy branch.

Start a slow
dance, lifting
a foot, planting
a heel to celebrate

greenness, rain
spatter on skin,
the humid pull
of the earth.

The whole world
turning in wet
and silence, a
damp mill wheel.

# 2

In silence and isolation, the dance begins. No one is meant
watch, least of all yourself. Hands fall to the sides, the head lo
empty, a broken stalk. The shoes fall away from the feet,
clothes peel away from the skin, body rags. The sight has slo
faded from your eyes, that sight of habit which sees nothi
Your ears buzz a little before they retreat to where the he
pulses, a soft drum. Then the dance begins, cleansing, heali
Through the bare forehead, along the bones of the feet, the ea
begins to speak. One knee lifts rustily, then the other. Tota
absent, you shuffle up and down, the purse of your loins strik
against your thighs, sperm and urine oozing down your lo
body like a gum. From where the legs join the rhythm sprea
upwards — the branch of the penis lifting, the cage of the r
whistling — to pass down the arms like electricity along a w
On the skin moisture forms, a wet leaf or a windbreath light a
mayfly. In wet and darkness you are reborn, the rain falling
your face as it would on a mossy tree trunk, wet hair clinging
your skull like bark, your breath mingling with the exhalati
of the earth, that eternal smell of humus and mould.

# 3

With a body
heavy as earth
she begins to speak;

her words
are dew, bright,
deadly to drink,

her hair,
the damp mare's
nest of the grass

her arms,
thighs, chance
of a swaying branch

her secret
message, shaped
by a wandering wind

puts the eye
of reason out;
so novice, blind,

ease your
hand into the
rot-smelling crotch

of a hollow
tree, and find
two pebbles of quartz

protected by
a spider's web:
her sunless breasts.

# 4

A circle of stones
surviving behind a
guttery farmhouse,

the capstone phallic
in a thistly meadow:
Seskilgreen Passage Grave.

Cup, circle,
triangle beating
their secret dance

(eyes, breasts,
thighs of a still
fragrant goddess).

I came last in May
to find the mound
drowned in bluebells

with a fearless wren
hoarding speckled eggs
in a stony crevice

while cattle
swayed sleepily
under low branches

lashing the ropes
of their tails
across the centuries.

# 5

Hinge of silence
     creak for us
Rose of darkness
     unfold for us
Wood anemone
     sway for us
Blue harebell
     bend to us
Moist fern
     unfurl for us
Springy moss
     uphold us
Branch of pleasure
     lean on us
Leaves of delight
     murmur for us
Odorous wood
     breathe on us
Evening dews
     pearl for us
Freshet of ease
     flow for us
Secret waterfall
     pour for us
Hidden cleft
     speak to us
Portal of delight
     inflame us
Hill of motherhood
     wait for us
Gate of birth
     open for us

*Snow curls in on the cold wind.*

Slowly, I push back the door.
After long absence, old habits
Are painfully revived, those disciplines
Which enable us to survive,
To keep a minimal fury alive
While flake by faltering flake

*Snow curls in on the cold wind.*

Along the courtyard, the boss
Of each cobblestone is rimmed
In white, with winter's weight
Pressing, like a silver shield,
On all the small plots of earth,
Inert in their living death as

*Snow curls in on the cold wind.*

Seized in a giant fist of frost,
The grounded planes at London Airport,
Mallarmé swans, trapped in ice.
The friend whom I have just left
Will be dead, a year from now,
Through her own fault, while

*Snow curls in on the cold wind.*

Or smothered by some glacial truth?
Thirty years ago, I learnt to reach
Across the rusting hoops of steel
That bound our greening waterbarrel
To save the living water beneath
The hardening crust of ice, before

*Snow curls in on the cold wind.*

But despair has a deeper crust.
In all our hours together, I never
Managed to ease the single hurt
That edged her towards her death;
Never reached through her loneliness
To save a trust, chilled after

*Snow curls in on the cold wind.*

I plunged through snowdrifts once,
Above our home, to carry
A telegram to a mountain farm.
Fearful but inviting, they waved me
To warm myself at the flaring
Hearth before I faced again where

*Snow curls in on the cold wind.*

The news I brought was sadness.
In a far city, someone of their name
Lay dying. The tracks of foxes,
Wild birds, as I climbed down
Seemed to form a secret writing
Minute and frail as life when

*Snow curls in on the cold wind.*

Sometimes, I know that message.
There is a disease called snow-sickness;
The glare from the bright god,
The earth's reply. As if that
Ceaseless, glittering light was
All the truth we'd left after

*Snow curls in on the cold wind.*

So, before dawn, comfort fails.
I imagine her end, in some sad
Bedsitting room, the steady hiss
Of the gas more welcome than an
Act of friendship, the protective
Oblivion of a lover's caress if

*Snow curls in on the cold wind.*

In the canyon of the street
The dark snowclouds hesitate,
Turning to slush almost before
They cross the taut canvas of
The street stalls, the bustle
Of a sweeper's brush after

*Snow curls in on the cold wind.*

The walls are spectral, white.
All the trees black-ribbed, bare.
Only veins of ivy, the sturdy
Laurel with its waxen leaves,
Its scant red berries, survive
To form a winter wreath as

*Snow curls in on the cold wind.*

What solace but endurance, kindness?
Against her choice, I still affirm
That nothing dies, that even from
Such bitter failure memory grows;
The snowflake's structure, fragile
But intricate as the rose when

*Snow curls in on the cold wind.*

Where I work
out of doors
children come
to present me
with an acorn,
a pine cone —
small secrets —

and a fat
grass snail
who uncoils
to carry his
whorled house
over the top
of my table.

With a pencil
I nudge him
back into
himself, but
fluid horns
unfurl, damp
tentacles, to

probe, test
space before
he drags his
habitation
forward again
on his single
muscular foot

rippling along
its liquid self-
creating path.
With absorbed,
animal faces
the children
watch us both

but he will
have none of
me, the static
angular world
of books, papers —
which is neither
green nor moist —

only to climb
around, over
as with rest-
less glistening
energy, he races
at full tilt
over the ledge

onto the grass.
All I am left
with is, between
pine cone & acorn,
the silver smear
of his progress
which will soon

wear off, like
the silvery galaxies,
mother of pearl
motorways, woven
across the grass
each morning by
the tireless snails

of the world,
minute as grains
of rice, gross
as conch or
triton, bequeath-
ing their shells
to the earth.

# 1

*Famine Cottage*

Soft flute note of absence;
Above MacCrystal's glen
Where shaggy gold of whin
Overhangs a hidden stream
I stumble upon a cabin,
Four crumbling walls and
A door, a shape easily
Rising from the ground,
As easily settling back:
Stones swathed in grass.

# 2

*Victorian Ireland*

Tennysonian solitudes of cliff
and waterfall —
silent, driving rain
clearing as sudden as it falls.
At the far end of the lake
a hunting lodge.
The black hoods of the carriages
outside the hall door
are spattered with rain.

I dwell in this leaky Western castle.
American matrons weave across the carpet,
Sorefooted as camels, and less useful.

Smooth Ionic columns hold up a roof.
A chandelier shines on a foxhound's coat:
The grandson of a grandmother I reared.

In the old days I read or embroidered,
But now it is enough to see the sky change,
Clouds extend or smother a mountain's shape.

Wet afternoons I ride in the Rolls;
Windshield wipers flail helpless against the rain:
I thrash through pools like smashing panes of glass.

And the light afterwards! Hedges steam,
I ride through a damp tunnel of sweetness,
The bonnet strewn with bridal hawthorn

From which a silver lady leaps, always young.
Alone, I hum with satisfaction in the sun,
An old bitch, with a warm mouthful of game.

# 1

*Back Door*

Oh, the wet melancholy
of morning fields! We
wake to a silence more
heavy than twilight
where an old car finds
its last life as a henhouse,
then falls apart slowly
before our eyes, dwindling
to a rust-gnawed fender
where a moulting hen
sits, one eye unlidding;
a mystic of vacancy.

# 2

*Kerry*

Shapes of pine and cypress
shade the hollow where
on thundery nights,
facing uphill, the
cattle sleep. Blossoms
of fuschia and yellow whin
drift slowly down upon
their fragrant, cumbersome
backs. Saga queens,
they sigh, knees
hidden in a carpet
of gold, flecked with
blue and scarlet.

*for Austin and Gerard Lynch*

Early summer, the upper bog,
slicing the thick, black turf,
spreading, footing, castling
and clamping, ritual skills
ruled by the sun's slow wheel
towards Knockmany, save when
a dark threat or spit of rain
raced us to shelter under
a tunnel damp corner
of the bank.
        At mealtimes
huge hobnails sparkled
a circle in the stiff grass
as we drank brown tea, bit
buttered planks of soda bread;
a messenger first, then helper,
I earned my right to sit among
the men for a stretch & smoke
while we put our heads together
in idle talk of neighbours
and weather.
        Almost a song
as we gathered ourselves again
and the flies spindled all
afternoon over the lukewarm
oily depths of the boghole
before we called quitting
time, stowed the flanged
spade, the squat turf barrow,
& tramped down the mountain
side, the sun over Knockmany,
old Lynch leading, home.

We match paces along the Hill Head Road,
the road to the old churchyard of Errigal Keerogue;
its early cross, a heavy stone hidden in grass.

As we climb, my old Protestant neighbour
signals landmarks along his well trodden path,
some hill or valley celebrated in local myth.

'Yonder's Whiskey Hollow,' he declares,
indicating a line of lunar birches.
We halt to imagine men plotting

against the wind, feeding the fire or
smothering the fumes of an old-fashioned worm
while the secret liquid bubbles & clears.

'And that's Foxhole Brae under there —'
pointing to the torn face of a quarry.
'It used to be crawling with them.'

(A red quarry slinks through the heather,
a movement swift as a bird's, melting as rain,
glimpsed behind a mound, disappears again.)

At Fairy Thorn Height the view fans out,
ruck and rise to where, swathed in mist
& rain, swells the mysterious saddle shape

of Knockmany Hill, its brooding tumulus
opening perspectives beyond our Christian myth.
'On a clear day you can see far into Monaghan.'

old Eagleson says, and we exchange sad notes
about the violence plaguing these parts;
last week, a gun battle outside Aughnacloy,

machine-gun fire splintering the wet thorns,
two men beaten up near dark Altamuskin,
an attempt to blow up Omagh Courthouse.

Helicopters overhead, hovering locusts.
Heavily booted soldiers probing vehicles, streets,
their strange antennae bristling, like insects.

At his lane's end, he turns to face me.
'Tell them down South that old neighbours
can still speak to each other around here'

& gives me his hand, but does not ask me in.
Rain misting my coat, I turn back towards
the main road, where cars whip smartly past

between small farms, fading back into forest.
Soon all our shared landscape will be effaced,
a quick stubble of pine recovering most.


WINDHARP

*for Patrick Collins*

The sounds of Ireland,
that restless whispering
you never get away
from, seeping out of
low bushes and grass,
heatherbells and fern,
wrinkling bog pools,
scraping tree branches,
light hunting cloud,
sound hounding sight,
a hand ceaselessly
combing and stroking
the landscape, till
the valley gleams
like the pile upon
a mountain pony's coat.

# THE CAVE OF NIGHT

*for Seán Lucy*

> *Men who believe in absurdities*
> *will commit atrocities.*
> — Voltaire

## 1

*Underside*

I have seen the high
vapour trails of the last
destroyers in dream:
I have seen the grey
underside of the moon
slide closer to earth...

## 2

*The Plain of Adoration*

*from the Irish, eleventh century*

Here was raised
a tall idol of savage fights:
the Cromm Cruaich —
the King Idol of Erin.

He was their Moloch,
this withered hump of mists,
hulking over every path,
refusing the eternal kingdom.

In a circle stood
four times three idols of stone:
to bitterly enslave his people,
the pivot figure was of gold.

In dark November,
when the two worlds near each other,
he glittered among his subjects,
blood-crusted, insatiable.

To him, without glory,
would they sacrifice their first-born:
with wailing and danger
pouring fresh blood for the Stooped One.

Under his shadow
they cried and mutilated their bodies:
from this worship of dolour
it is called the Plain of Adoration.

Well born Gaels lay prostrate
beneath his crooked shape until
gross and glittering as a cinema organ
he sank back into his earth.

# 3

*Cave*

The rifled honeycomb
of the high-rise hotel
where a wind tunnel moans.
While jungleclad troops
ransack the Falls, race
through huddled streets,
we lie awake, the wide
window washed with rain,
your oval face, and tide
of yellow hair luminous
as you turn to me again
seeking refuge as the
cave of night blooms
with fresh explosions.

# 4

*All Night*

All night spider webs
of nothing. Condemned to
that treadmill of helplessness.
Distended, drowning fish,
frogs with lions' jaws.
A woman breasted butterfly
copulates with a dying bat.
A pomegranate bursts slowly
between her ladyship's legs.
Her young peep out
with bared teeth:
the eggs of hell
fertilizing the abyss.

Frail skyscrapers incline
together like stilts.
Grain elevators melt.
Cities subside as liners
leave by themselves,
all radios playing.
A friendly hand places
a warm bomb under
the community centre
where the last evacuees
are trying a hymn.
Still singing, they
part for limbo, still
tucking their blankets
over separating limbs.

A land I did not seek
to enter. Pure terror.
Ice floes sail past
grandly as battleships.
Blue gashed arctic distances
ache the retina and
the silence grows to
a sparkle of starlight —
sharpened knives.
Lift up your telescope,
old colonel, and learn
to lurch with the penguins!
In the final place
a solitary being begins
its slow dance. . . .

# 5

*Falls Funeral*

Unmarked faces
fierce with grief

a line of children
led by a small coffin

the young
mourning the young

a sight beyond tears
beyond pious belief

David's brethren
in the Land of Goliath.


# 6

*Ratonnade*

Godoi, godoi, godoi!
Our city burns & so did Troy,
Finic, Finic, marsh birds cry
As bricks assemble a new toy.

    Godoi, godoi, godoi.

Humble mousewives crouch in caves,
Monster rats lash their tails,
Cheese grows scarce in Kingdom Come,
Rodents leap to sound of drum.

    Godoi, godoi, godoi.

Civilisation slips & slides when
Death sails past with ballroom glide:
Tangomaster of the skulls whose
Harvest lies in griefs & rues.

    Godoi, godoi, godoi.

On small hillsides darkens fire,
Wheel goes up, forgetting tyre,
Grudgery holds its winter court,
Smash and smithereens to report.

    Godoi, godoi, godoi.

Against such horrors hold a cry,
Sweetness mothers us to die,
Wisens digs its garden patch,
Silence lifts a silver latch.

    Godoi, godoi, godoi.

Mingle musk love-birds say,
Honey-hiving all the day,
Ears & lips & private parts,
Muffled as the sound of carts.

    Godoi, godoi, godoi.

Moral is of worsens hours,
Cripple twisting only flowers,
One arm lost, one leg found,
Sad men fall on common ground.

Godoi!

The noise.

He was pulled out, squealing,
an iron cleek sunk in the roof
of his mouth.

(Don't say they are not intelligent:
they know the hour has come
and they want none of it;
they dig in their little trotters,
will not go dumb or singing
to the slaughter.)

That high pitched final effort,
no single sound could match it —

a big plane roaring off,
a *diva* soaring towards her last note,
the brain-chilling persistence of an electric saw,
scrap being crushed.

Piercing & absolute,
only high heaven ignores it.

Then a full stop.
Mickey Boyle plants
a solid thump of the mallet
flat between the ears.

Swiftly the knife seeks the throat;
swiftly the other cleavers work
till the carcass is hung up
shining and eviscerated as
a surgeon's coat.

A child is given
the bladder to play with.
But the walls of the farmyard
still hold that scream,
are built around it.

*When dining they all sit not on chairs, but on the ground,
strewing beneath them wolf- or dog-skins. . . . Beside
them are the hearths blazing with fire, with cauldrons
and spits with great pieces of meat; brave warriors are
honoured by the finest portions.*

— Diodorus Siculus

I

A steaming hunk of meat
landed before him —

it was red & running
with blood & his stomach

rose & fell to see it
his juices churned to meet it
his jaws opened to chew it

cracking & splitting down
to the marrow stuffed bone
which he licked & sucked

as clean as a whistle

before he sighed 'Enough!'
and raised his gold ringed arms

to summon one
of the waiting women
to squat across his lap

while the musician pulled
his long curved nails
through the golden hair
of his harp.

II

*What song to sing?*
the blind man said:

*sing the hero*
*who lost his head*

*sing the hero*
*who lopped it off*

*sing the torso*
*still propped aloft*

*sing the nobles*
*who judged that fall*

*sing the sword*
*so fierce & tall*

*sing the ladies*
*whose bowels crave*

*its double edge*
*of birth & grave.*

III

Timbers creak
in the banquet hall;
the harper's fingers
are ringed with blood
& the ornate battle sword
sheathed in its scabbard.
The king has fallen asleep
under the weight of his crown
while in the corner a hound
& bitch are quarrelling
over the hero's bone.

## HUNTER'S WEAPON

'Huzza,' you cried, seeing a leg
leap into the air, like a hat,
a baseball or cricket bat
hurled high after a home run,
a long drawn but winning game

& then you realised it was your own
and sat down
awkwardly
sideways, to cry
among the other dying men

which you did not, and now
wooden-legged, piratical,
you thump around your Paris flat to tell
how many toothsome ladies fell
for your game leg

'They beg
to handle it,' you say,
and wake to find it dangling —
a hunter's weapon —
around their bedpost
at peep of day.


## THE MASSACRE

Two crows flap to a winter wood.
Soldiers with lances and swords
Probe the entrails of innocents.
A burgomeister washes manicured
Hands before mourning citizens.
The snow on the gable is linen crisp,
That on the ground laced with blood.
Two crows flap to a winter wood.

282

The mother cat
opens her claws
like petals

bends her spine
to expose her
battery of tits

where her young
toothless snouts
screwed eyes

on which light
cuffs mild
paternal blows

jostle & cry
for position
except one

so boneless
& frail it
pulls down

air, not milk.
Wan little scut,
you are already

set for death,
never getting
a say against

the warm circle
of your mother's
breast, as she

arches voluptuously
in the pleasure
of giving life

to those who
claim it, bit-
ten navel cords

barely dried,
already fierce
at the trough.

*for Eileen Carney*

We hesitate along
flower-encumbered

avenues of the dead;
Greek, Puerto-Rican,

Italian, Irish —
(our true Catholic

world, a graveyard)
but a squirrel

dances us to it
through the water

sprinklered grass,
collapsing wreaths,

& taller than you
by half, lately from

that hidden village
where you were born

I sway with you
in a sad, awkward

dance of pain
over the grave of

my uncle & namesake —
the country fiddler —

& the grave of almost
all your life held,

your husband & son
all three sheltering

under the same
squat, grey stone.

❧

You would cry out
against what has

happened, such
heedless hurt,

had you the harsh
nature for it

(swelling the North
wind with groans,

curses, imprecations
against heaven's will)

but your mind is
a humble house, a

soft light burning
beneath the holy

picture, the image
of the seven times

wounded heart of
her, whose portion

is to endure.  For
there is no end

to pain, nor of
love to match it

& I remember Anne
meekest of my aunts

rocking and praying
in her empty room.

Oh, the absurdity
of grief in that

doll's house, all
the chair legs sawn

to nurse dead children:
love's museum!

∾

It sent me down
to the millstream

to spy upon a
mournful waterhen

shushing her young
along the autumn

flood, as seriously
as a policeman and

after scampering
along, the proud

plumed squirrel
now halts, to stand

at the border
of this grave plot

serious, still,
a small ornament

holding something,
a nut, a leaf —

like an offering
inside its paws.

∾

For an instant
you smile to see

his antics, then
bend to tidy

flowers, gravel,
like any woman

making a bed,
arranging a room,

over what were
your darlings' heads

and far from
our supposed home

I submit again
to stare soberly

at my own name
cut on a gravestone

& hear the creak
of a ghostly fiddle

filter through
American earth

the slow pride
of a lament.

ALL SOULS

I

All the family are together.
A yellow glass of whiskey punch in one hand,
John Joe is rehearsing his oldest joke;
He whinnies into laughter a head
Before the others.
                    His bald spot glistens
And the pates of half of those listening,
Eager to assist out his say, to get
Their own oar in —
                    human warmth!
The details of the room hardly matter,
The stuffed cock pheasant, the photo
Of Uncle James at the World's Fair,
Three smiling nuns. That polite, parlour
Coldness, stale air, and dying armchairs.
And the dusty silence of the piano lid
Which has not been lifted since Auntie died:
An ebony glitter.
                    God rest her,
A dead hand runs down the scales,
*Diminuendo.* And Uncle James wanders in,
Tapping the hall barometer with his fingernail,
Fussily, before he appears,
                    a decent skeleton.

II

Now the dead and their descendants
Share in the necessary feast of blood.
A child's voice trembles into song,
A warm sphere suspended in light.
The knuckles lifting the clove-scented glass
To your lips are also branched with bone
So toast your kin in the chill oblong
Of the gilt mirror where the plumage
Of a shot bird still swells chestnut brown.

*To have gathered from the air a live tradition.*
— Ezra Pound

*Roving, unsatisfied ghost,*
*old friend, lean closer;*
*leave us your skills:*
*lie still in the quiet*
*of your chosen earth.*


## 1

*Woodtown Manor, Again*

We vigil by the dying fire,
talk stilled for once,
foil clash of rivalry,
fierce Samurai pretence.

Outside a rustle of bramble,
jack fox around the framing
elegance of a friend's house
we both choose to love:

two natives warming ourselves
at the revived fire
in a high-ceilinged room
worthy of Carolan —

clatter of harpsichord
the music leaping
like a long candle flame
to light ancestral faces

pride of music
pride of race

## 2

Abruptly, closer to self-revelation
than I have ever seen, you speak;
bubbles of unhappiness breaking
the bright surface of 'Till Eulenspiegel'.

'I am in great danger,' you whisper,
as much to the failing fire
as to your friend & listener;
'though, you have great luck'.

Our roles reversed, myself cast
as the light-fingered master,
the lucky dancer on thin ice,
rope walker on his precipice.

## 3

I sense the magisterial strain
behind your jay's laugh,
ruddy moustached, smiling,
your sharp player's mask.

Instinct wrung and run
awry all day, powers idled
to self-defeat, the vacuum
behind the catalyst's gift.

Beyond the flourish
of personality, peacock
pride of music or language:
a constant, piercing torment!

Signs earlier, a stranger
made to stumble at a bar door,
fatal confusion of the powers
of the upper and lower air.

A playing with fire, leading
you, finally, tempting you
to a malevolence, the
calling of death for another.

## 4

A door opens,
and she steps into the room,
smothered in a black gown,
harsh black hair falling to her knees,
a pallid tearstained face.

*How pretty you look,*
*Miss Death!*

# 5

*Samhain*

Sing a song
for the mistress
of the bones

the player
on the black keys
the darker harmonies

light jig
of shoe buckles
on a coffin lid

∾

Harsh glint
of the wrecker's lantern
on a jagged cliff

across the ceaseless
glitter of the spume:
a seagull's creak.

The damp-haired
seaweed-stained sorceress
marshlight of defeat

∾

Chill of winter
a slowly failing fire
faltering desire

Darkness of Darkness
we meet on our way
in loneliness

Blind Carolan
Blind Raftery
Blind Tadgh

# 6

*Hell Fire Club*

Around the house all night
dark music of the underworld,
hyena howl of the unsatisfied,
latch creak, shutter sigh,
the groan and lash of trees,
a cloud upon the moon.

Released demons moan.
A monstrous black tom
*couchant* on the roofbeam.
The widowed peacock screams
knowing the fox's tooth:
a cry, like rending silk,

& a smell of carrion where
baulked of their prey,
from pane to tall window
pane, they flit, howling
to where he lies, who has
called them from defeat.

Now, their luckless meat,
turning a white pillowed room,
smooth as a bridal suite
into a hospital bed where
a lucid beast fights against
a blithely summoned doom.

At the eye of the storm
a central calm, where
tearstained, a girl child
sleeps cradled in my arms
till the morning points
and you are gone.

# 7

*The Two Gifts*

And a nation mourns:
The blind horseman with his harp-carrying servant,
Hurrying through darkness to a great house
Where a lordly welcome waits, as here:
Fingernail spikes in candlelight recall
A ripple & rush of upland streams,
The slant of rain on void eye sockets,
The shrill of snipe over mountains
Where a few stragglers nest in bracken —
After Kinsale, after Limerick, after Aughrim,
After another defeat, to be redeemed
By the curlew sorrow of an aisling.

*The little Black Rose*
*(To be sprinkled with tears)*
*The Silk of the Kine*
*(To be shipped as dead meat)*

*'They tore out my tongue*
*So I grew another one,'*
*I heard a severed head*
*Sing down a bloody stream.*

But a lonelier lady mourns,
the muse of a man's particular gift,
Mozart's impossible marriage of fire & ice,
skull sweetness of the last quartets,
Mahler's horn wakening the autumn forest,
the harsh blood pulse of Stravinsky,
the hammer of Boulez
                which you will never lift.

Never to be named with your peers,
'I am in great danger,' he said;
firecastles of flame,
a name extinguished.

# 8

*Lament*

With no family
& no country

a voice rises
out of the threatened beat
of the heart & the brain cells

(not for the broken people
nor for the blood soaked earth)

a voice
like an animal howling
to itself on a hillside
in the empty church of the world

a lament so total
it mourns no one
but the globe itself
turning in the endless halls

of space, populated
with passionless stars

and that always raised voice

*1972-1974*

In their houses beneath the sea
the salmon glide, in human form.

They assume their redgold skin
to mount the swollen stream,

Wild in the spawning season;
a shining sacrifice for men!

So throw back these bones again:
they will flex alive, grow flesh

When the ruddy salmon returns,
a lord to his underwater kingdom.

## UP SO DOÜN

I open underwater eyes
and the great lost world
of the primordial drifts
a living thicket of coral
a darting swarm of fish

> *(or the moon with an apron*
> *of iceblue tinted cloud,*
> *rust bright Mars or Saturn's*
> *silvery series of spheres)*

how quiet it is down here
where wandering minnows explore
the twin doors of my eyelids
lip silently against my mouth

> *(how still it is up here*
> *where I dance quietly to myself,*
> *stilt across a plain, hardly*
> *disturbing the dust on the moon's shelf)*

I had forgotten that we live between
gasps of, glimpses of miracle;
once sailed through the air like birds,
walked in the waters like fish.


## SPRINGS

> *for Ted Hughes*

> Dying, the salmon
> heaves up its head
> in the millstream.
> Great sores ring
> its gills, its eyes,
> a burning rust
> slowly corrodes
> the redgold skin.

Great river king,
nearby the Nore pours
over foaming weirs
its light and music,
endlessly dissolving
walls into webs of
water that drift away
among slow meadows.

But you are abdicating,
you are yielding,
no fight left but in
the hinge of your jaws,
(the hook or *kype*)
gasping, clasping
for a last breath
of this soiled kingdom.

Prince of ocean, from
what shared springs
we pay you homage
we have long forgotten
but I mourn your passing
and would erase
from this cluttered earth
our foul disgrace:

Drain the poison
from the streams,
cleanse the enormous
belly of ocean, tear
those invisible miles
of mesh so that your
kin may course again
through clear waters.

The world we see only shadows
what was there. So a dead man
fables in your chair, or stands
in the space your table now holds.
Over your hearth the sea hisses
and a storm wind harshly blows.
Before your eyes the red sandstone
of the wall crumbles, weed run wild
where three generations ago
a meadow climbed, above a city
which now slowly multiplies,
its gaunt silos, fuming mills,
strange to the first inhabitants
as Atlantis to a fish's eyes.

*Grattan Hill, 1974*


## HEARTH SONG

*for Seamus Heaney*

I

The Nialls' cottage had one:
it lived under a large flagstone,
loving the warmth of the kitchen.

Chill or silent, for whole days,
it would, all of a sudden, start
its constant, compelling praise.

And all of us, dreaming or chatting
over the fire, would go quiet,
harkening to that insistent creak,

Accustoming ourselves all over again
to that old, but always strange, sound,
coming at us from under the ground,

Rising from beneath our feet,
welling up out of the earth,
a solitary, compulsive song

Composed for no one, a tune
dreamt up under a flat stone,
earth's fragile, atonal rhythm.

II

And did I once glimpse one?
I call up that empty farmhouse,
its blind, ghostly audience

And a boy's bare legs dangling
down from a stool, as he peers
through a crack in the flagstones

And here it strikes up again,
that minute, manic cellist,
scraping the shape of itself,

Its shining, blue-black back
and pulsing, tendril limbs
throbbing and trembling in darkness

a hearth song of happiness.

# 1

*Brigid Montague (1876-1966)*

A hand pushes back a strand of grey hair.
All day people come to complain and take.
She stands at her desk, signing, listening;
Old-fashioned wire-rimmed spectacles glint.
Worn rights of way to well or bog,
Protracted, hurtful family quarrels,
The resentment of the trapped animal,
Shouldering others on their narrow path;
To bear that always renewed burden,
The tuneless cries of the self-absorbed,
And stand patient, serving under the yoke,
Never complaining; always ready to assist.
Bow down, for your own sake, before the good,
Their sweet assurance, taken for granted.

# 2

*Winifred Montague (1900-1983)*

Old girl courier of Cumann na mBan,
Even before you died you were on cloud nine,
Squatting like an effigy of yourself
In your comfortable rocking chair
With an aureole of white, wispy hair.
Not a sign of contrariness, of bad temper
Anywhere! Faltering old neighbours or
Protestants you rarely had a good word for
Greeted with benevolence; or benign indifference?
On the mantelpiece burly Pope John Paul
Shared his public place of honour
With your life's monarch: the Queen Mother.
Such rich acceptance might take care
Of our little local spot of bother.

## SEMIOTICS

Loudest of all our protests when
the Deaf Mute Club of Ireland gather
to honour a brother, slammed down
by an abrupt bullet, near his Council home.
Challenged, he could only wave to answer
some tense and trigger-happy soldier.
Upon the broad British Embassy steps
the spokesman of the Deaf Mutes
makes an impassioned, fiery speech
in sign language. Fierce applause.
What officials spy through windows
of those comfortable Georgian rooms
is a flickering semaphore of fingers,
then an angry swirl of palms.


## CASSANDRA'S ANSWER

I

All I can do is curse, complain.
I told you the flames would come
and the small towns blaze. Though

Precious little you did about it!
Obdurate. Roots are obstructions
as well as veins of growth.

How my thick tongue longs
for honey's ease, the warm
full syllables of praise

Instead of this gloomy procession
of casualties, clichés of decease;
deaf mutes' clamouring palms.

To have one subject only,
fatal darkness of prophecy,
gaunt features always veiled.

301

I have forgotten how I sang
as a young girl, before my voice
changed, and I tolled funerals.

I feel my mouth grow heavy again,
a storm cloud is sailing in;
a street will receive its viaticum

in the fierce release of a bomb.
*Goodbye, Main Street, Fintona,*
*goodbye to the old Carney home.*

II

To step inside a childhood home,
tattered rafters that the dawn
leaks through, brings awareness

Bleaker than any you have known.
Whole albums of Births, Marriages,
roomfuls of tears and loving confidences

Gone as if the air has swallowed them;
stairs which climb towards nothing,
walls hosed down to flaking stone:

you were born inside a skeleton.

REAL IRISHMAN

On St Patrick's Day, Billy Davidson cried,
Big and blubbering, by the rock garden.
The master had ordered him to play outside,
Snapping, 'You're not a real Irishman,
You're a Protestant'. I slip out to comfort
Big Billy, chance an arm around him.
'What does it matter, your religion —
Some people still call me the American! —
What counts most is, you're my friend.'
Decades later, in a dark pub, after hours,
A swirl of trouble with two off-duty U.D.R.
Suddenly in the background, a rough voice roars:
'John Montague is my old friend and neighbour;
Lay a hand on him and you deal with Billy Davidson'.

Thady, sixty years out of Donegal,
propped, overflowing his tall barstool,
my father's pal, the last, hollering:

'Jim was a decent man, he prayed every night
for his family; I'm glad to meet his son.
Sure, he took the drop, but never gave in.'

(They shared a horsebox in a Brooklyn slum,
a boarding house run by rheumatic Mrs Averril
who pitted her rosary against the Atom Bomb.)

'But your uncle was a right whoremaster,
riding black women.' Monaghan's father
snorts in the background, 'Keep the party clean.'

Just as our ears were beginning to burn!
Thady, an old motor man, reverses gears,
rewinding the spool of those solitary years

To recall a summer evening in Donegal,
how he won the raffle in the Parish Hall.
First prize: a kiss from the prettiest girl.

His eyes moisten, his voice thickens,
he lays aside his daily, *Journal American*,
'I can still picture her shy expression.'

Among gasoline fumes, run-down brownstones,
Thady still holds on to his lucky number,
waiting stolidly on the platform beside her,

How when he kissed her, there was a cheer.
'The one time in my whole life.' Thoughtfully,
Thady looks back down into his chilled beer.

'But I have always respected women.
So did your father.' The stale odour
of lives broken down, next to nothing,

yet, on the litter, that stray offering.

HUSBANDRY

*for Derry Jeffares*

Because you were barren,
male by male tree, or
one female by another,
I had to cut you down.
A hard task, kneeling with
the saw's serrated blade,

To scythe thick grass,
seek out your smothered side.
Close to earth as possible,
the gardening manual said;
a neighbouring apple tree
shook petals on my head —
to see an old neighbour
so roughly treated?

A bird called and called,
balanced upon a thorn,
a spider crawled upon
my sweating hand until
the foot was sawn, and
all your branching platform

Swayed: but still held on.
I had to put both arms
around your lean waist
to tug you finally down.
No damp pith spirted,
but that raw stump shone.

We part the leaves.

Small, squat, naked
Jim Toorish stood in
the churning middle
of Clarkes' turnhole.

Black hair on his poll,
a roll of black hair
over his stomach, that
strange tussock below.

With a rib of black
fur along his back
from thick neckbone
to simian buttocks.

From which — *inescapable* —
his father root sprang,
gross as a truncheon,
normal as a pump-handle.

And cheerfully splashing,
scooping chill waters over
his curls, his shoulders —
*that hairy thing*!

To cleanse everything
but our prurient giggling
which took long years
for me to exorcise

Until I saw him again,
upright and glorious,
a satyr, laughing in
the spray at Florence.

The bloody tent-flap opens. We slide
into life, slick with slime and blood.
Cunt, or Cymric *cwm*, Chaucerian *quente*,
the first home from which man is sent
into banishment, to spend his whole life
cruising to return, raising a puny mast
to sail back into those moist lips
that overhang *labia minora* and *clitoris*.
To sigh and die upon the Mount of Venus,
layer after layer of warm moss,
to return to that first darkness!
Small wonder she grins at us, from gable
or church wall. For the howling babe
life's warm start: man's question mark.

GABRIEL

To encounter an archangel
demands no preparation, although
frail the will, weak the vessel.
You hardly notice his wings,
falcon wide, or warmly folded,
for he was always expected. And
your healed heart trembles.
'In the teeth of the hurricane,
sing sweetness,' he announces,
'in the pitch of this darkness,
sing tenderness,' and if you will,
as omen for the imminent world,
'sing peace.' The dove's breast
stirs in the savour of his presence.

307

Night after night
we lay, embracing,
under the shadows
of Sir John's Castle.

Or in the hedge
by the lodge gates —
Maureen Canavan —
arms straining

towards a freedom
neither of us felt
willing to mention:
abhorred temptation!

Hugging and kissing
but holding our lower
parts separate and
rigid as gateposts

leading to adventures
we could never enter
blithely together;
love's untilled estate

in moonlight around us,
from cobwebbed cellars
the mocking laughter
of a ghostly landlord.

Tonguetied I felt
you drift away, with
nothing done or said,
only the lost fragrance

of your fair head —
*ceannbhán*, a bog blossom —
on warm summer evenings
along the Waterside

or bent towards mine
in Glencull choir
as the handbell shivers
*O Salutaris Hostia.*

## DEER PARK

A flourish of silver
trumpets as the royal
favourite is prepared
for the swansdown bed.

Fingers and toes
palpable, succulent
as those pert curves
of mouth, snub nose.

The string of pearls
on her stomach folds
luminously pendent
like rare raindrops

While a pair of pure-
bred hunting hounds
snuffle her plump
and perfumed hands.

A candid light streams
from such guileless,
dimpled nakedness, such
cherubic openness!

And the fillet of
gold she bears so
demurely in honour
of her sovereign master,

Upon her piled strands
of auburn Irish hair,
looped to reveal her
golden neck collar.

A king's treasure
of roseate flesh
caught on canvas
for a king's pleasure

With a full quiver
of arrows, a dangling
brace of pheasant
all stamped: royal property.


MATINS

That final bright morning you climb
The stairs to my balcony bed,
Unasked; unashamed: naked.
Barely a please was said
But in the widening light
Our bodies linked, blazed,
Our spirits melded. The dawn
Of a capital city swarmed
Beneath us, but we were absorbed,
Your long hair tenting your head,
Your body taut as a divining rod.
There is in such exchanges a harvest,
A source or wellspring of sweetness,
Grace beyond sense, body's intelligence.

Your lithe and golden body
haunts me, as I haunt you:
corsairs with different freights
who may only cross by chance
    on lucky nights.

So our moorings differ.
But scents of your pleasure
still linger disturbingly
around me: fair winds or
    squalls of danger?

There is a way of forgetting you,
but I have forgotten it:
prepared wildly to cut free,
to lurch, like a young man,
    towards ecstasy!

Nightly your golden body turns
and turns in my shuddering dream.
Why is the heart never still,
yielding again to the cardinal
    lure of the beautiful?

Age should bring its wisdom
but in your fragrant presence
my truths are one, swirling
to a litany — sweet privateer —
    of grateful adulation.

That first wild summer
we watched each other,
my greying hair and
wary eyes slowly drawn
to be warmed by your
flaring hair, abundant body.

No ice princess, you call
me down from my high tower —
on our first night together
I awoke, to watch over
your rich shape, a shower
of gold in the moonlight.

And an old fable stirred:
a stag rising from a wet brake —
Danae deluged by Zeus?
Rather, youth's promise fulfilled,
homely as a harvest field
from my Tyrone childhood

Where I hoist warm sheaves
to tent them into golden stooks,
each detail, as I wade
through the moonlit stubble,
crayon bright, as in
a child's colouring-book.

I

There is a white light in the room.
It is anger. He is angry, or
She is angry, or both are angry.
To them it is absolute, total,
It is everything; but to the visitor,
The onlooker, the outsider,
It is the usual, the absurd;
For if they did not love each other
Why should they heed a single word?

II

Another sad goodbye at the airport;
Neither has much to say, *en garde*,
Lest a chance word turn barbed.
You bring me, collect me, each journey
Not winged as love, but heavy as duty;
Lohengrin's swan dipping to Charon's ferry.

III

A last embrace at the door,
Your lovely face made ugly
By a sudden flush of tears
Which tell me more than any phrase,
Tell me what I most need to hear,
Wash away and cleanse my fears:
You have never ceased to love me.

To wake up and discover —
a *splairge* of chill water —
that she was but a forthright woman
on whom we had bestowed
(because of the crook of an elbow,
the swing of a breast or hip,
a glance, half-understood)
divinity or angelhood?

Raised by the fury of our need,
supplicating, lusting, grovelling
before the tall tree of Artemis
the transfiguring bow of Diana,
the rooting vulva of Circe, or
the slim shape of a nymph,
luring, dancing, beckoning:
all her wild disguises!

And now she does not shine,
or ride, like the full moon,
gleam or glisten like cascades
of uncatchable, blinding water;
disturb, like the owl's cry,
predatory, hovering: marshlight,
moonstone, or devil's daughter,
but conducts herself like any

Ordinary citizen, orderly or slattern,
giving us a piece of her mind,
pacifying or scolding children,
or, more determinedly, driving
or riding to her office, after
depositing the children in a *crêche*,
while she fulfills herself,
competing with the best.

Of course, she is probably saying
the same thing of us, as Oisín,
our tall hero from Fairyland,
descends or falls from the saddle
to dwindle into an irritable husband,
worn down by the quotidian,

unwilling to transform the night
with love's necessary shafts of light.

Except that when the old desires stir —
fish under weed-tangled waters —
will she remember that we once were
the strange ones who understood
the powers that coursed so furiously
through her witch blood, prepared
to stand, bareheaded, open handed,
to recognise, worship and obey:

To defy custom, redeem the ordinary,
with trembling heart and obeisant knee
to kneel, prostrate ourselves again,
if necessary, before the lady?


SHE CRIES

    She puts her face against the wall
and cries, crying for herself,
crying for our children, crying
for all of us
              in this strange age
of shrinking space, with the needle
of Concorde saluting Mount Gabriel
with its supersonic boom, soaring
from London or Paris to Washington,
a slender, metallic, flying swan

and all the other paraphernalia, hidden
missiles hoarded in silos, bloated
astronauts striding the dusty moon,
and far beyond, our lonely message,
that long probe towards Venus

but most of all for her husband
she cries, against the wall,
the poet at his wooden desk,
that toad with a jewel in his head,
no longer privileged, but still
trying to crash, without faltering,
the sound barrier, the dying word.

315

I

She wakes in a hand-painted cot,
chats and chortles to herself,
a healthy small being, a happy elf,
sister to the early train whistle,
the bubbling dawn chorus along
the wisteria of Grattan Hill.

No complaints as yet, enjoying
through curtains the warm sunlight,
until she manages to upend herself.
Then the whine starts. Is it anger
or lust for the bottle?

Lift her up, warm and close
or held at arm's length —
that smell, like a sheep pen,
a country hedge steaming after rain.

As the bottle warms, the decibels increase,
the scaldie's mouth gapes open;
head numb, coated tongue,
cortex ends squealing, no
thirsty drunk at a bar,
nursing a hangover, manages such concentration.

Daughter, dig in, with fists like ferns
unfurling, to basic happiness!
Little one, you are now
nothing but the long music of the gut,
a tug of life, with halts
for breathing, stomach swelling.

II

On your throne afterwards
bang your heels, examine your new
and truly wonderful hands,
try out, warm up, your
little runs of satisfaction.

Day by day, they also grow,
sound experiments in the laboratory
of the self, animal happiness,
the tonal colour of rage, cartoon
attempts to communicate, eyes beaming,
burbles rising. Best of all when

like any bird or beast waking,
you wail to yourself, with whoops,
finger stuffed gurgles, and my reward
for the morning, your speciality
(after the peristaltic hiccup)
when you smile and squeal with
sudden, sharp whistles —
O my human kettle!

She brings us to her secret place, behind the apple tree, on tl
last terrace of our garden. Ordering her little friends bossil
she leads them first up the ladder; we follow behind, bashf
giants. She has set up a table, a few boards balanced on stone
where a half-broken doll sits facing a bruised teddy. One l
one, large and small, we are assigned our places: 'now *you* s
there' and '*you* sit here'. Then a fresh batch of orders arrive
'Since I'm the Mummy I pour out the tea.' A child's har
reaches out, plucks and distributes china cups so delicate th
they are invisible. Then it grasps a teapot handle out of spa
and leans across to each of us in turn, before settling back th
solid object made of air down in front of her. 'And here are tl
sandwiches and biscuits.' Each of us receives a dusty twig
leaf. 'Now you all eat up and if any of you complain I'll te
Daddy on you.' She gives Teddy an affectionate poke whic
sends him sprawling to the ground. 'And sit up straight: r
slouching when we have visitors.' Solemnly, we lift the cups
our lips, toasting each other silently. Through the branches
the apple tree we can see the city, a pall of smoke over tl
docks, the opaque matte surface of the River Lee. Beyor
those small hills is the airport and as we drink invisibility
plane climbs, a sliver of silver in the sunlight. Filtered throug
the apple blossom its sound is as distant and friendly as tl
hum of a honey-seeking bee.

My daughter, Úna, wanders
off to play in the forest,
unafraid, her new rag doll
clutched under one arm:
a small fairy queen, trail-
ed by her elderly knight.

At the centre, I find her
beneath black hemlock, red cedar,
halted on a carpet, a compost
of fallen leaves, rusty haws
and snowberries, knobbly chestnuts:
decay's autumnal weft.

She has found a dead bird
which she holds up in her
other hand; eyes, bright beads,
but the long beak spiky, cold,
twig legs crisped inwards.
*Why not fly?* she demands

And as I kneel to explain
(taking the retted corpse away)
*dead*, she repeats, puzzled.
So we bury the scant body
under a mound of damp leaves,
a gnome's pyre, a short barrow:

Her first funeral ceremony.
*Home now*, I nudge gently,
past the slapping branches,
the shallow Pacific rain pools
she loves ploutering through
in her diminutive wellingtons.

Beyond the tall woods, lights
of Victoria are flickering on:
yellow flares of sodium
under dark coastal clouds
crossing Vancouver Island;
dream cattle swaying home.

## NEST

When all the birds
     in the nest are there,
is that the start
     of a new despair?


## THE BLACK LAKE

Across the black lake
Two figures row their boat
With slow, leaning strokes.
The grind of their rowlocks
Is rhythmic as a heartbeat.

Seven stooks stand
In a moonwashed field —
Seven pillars of gold —
While, beyond, two haystacks
Roped down to the earth.

Three lean cattle munch
The heavy aftergrass, or
Raise their heads towards
A stonewalled corner where
A couple lean from each other.

The moon climbs the hill.
The night brims with light,
A pantry, silent with milk.
The rowers reach the cottage,
The couple do not speak.

## LUGGALA

*for Garech Browne*

Again and again in dream, I return to that shore. There is a wind
rising, a gull is trying to skim over the pines, and the waves
whisper and strike along the bright sickle of the little strand.
Shoving through reeds and rushes, leaping over a bogbrown
stream, I approach the temple by the water's edge, death's
shrine, cornerstone of your sadness. I stand inside, by one of the
pillars of the mausoleum, and watch the water in the stone
basin. As the wind ruffles cease, a calm surface appears, like a
mirror or crystal. And into it your face rises, sad beyond speech,
sad with an acceptance of blind, implacable process. For by
this grey temple are three tombs, a baby brother, a half-sister
and a grown brother, killed at twenty-one. Their monuments of
Wicklow granite are as natural here as the scattered rocks, but
there is no promise of resurrection, only the ultimate silence of
the place, the shale littered face of the scree, the dark, dark
waters of the glacial lake.

## SURVIVOR

Under his high cliff, Fintan waited.
He watched as the floods rose, rose,
Never fell. He heard the women wail,
Wail, and accept. He felt the change
Through his nostrils, flattening to gills,
His arms thinning to fins, his torso
Tightening into a single thrash:
The undulating flail of a great fish.

Nothing human would last. For centuries
He slept at the bottom of the world,
Currents stroking his sleek, strong back.
Slowly, the old bare earth reappeared,
Barren, but with a rainbow brightened.
Life might begin again. He lunges upwards.

I

The eagle looked at this changing world;
sighed and disappeared into the mountain.

Before he left he had a last reconnoitre:
the multi-coloured boats in the harbour

nodded their masts and a sandy white
crescent of strand smiled back at him.

How he liked the slight, drunk lurch
of the fishing fleet, the tide hoist-

ing them a little, at their ropes' end.
Beyond, wrack, and the jutting rocks

emerging, slowly, monsters stained
and slimed with strands of seaweed.

Ashore, beached boats and lobster-
pots, settled as hens in the sand.

II

Content was life in its easiest form;
another was the sudden growling storm

which the brooding eagle preferred,
bending his huge wings into the winds'

wild buffeting, or thrusting down along
the wide sky, at an angle, slideways

to survey the boats, scurrying homewards,
tacking against the now contrary winds,

all of whom he knew by their names.
To be angry in the morning, calmed

by midday, but brooding again in
the evening was all in a day's quirk

with lengthy intervals for silence,
gliding along, like a blessing, while

the fleet toiled on earnestly beneath
him, bulging with a fine day's catch.

### III

But now he had to enter the mountain.
Why? Because a cliff had asked him?

The whole world was changing, with one
language dying; and another encroaching,

bright with buckets, cries of children.
There seemed to be no end to them,

and the region needed a guardian —
so the mountain had told him. And

a different destiny lay before him:
to be the spirit of that mountain.

Everyone would stand in awe of him.
When he was wrapped in the mist's caul

they would withdraw because of him,
peer from behind blind or curtain.

When he lifted his wide forehead
bold with light, in the morning,

they would all laugh and smile with him.
It was a greater task than an eagle's

aloofness, but sometimes, under his oilskin
of coiled mist, he sighs for lost freedom.

I

From the platform
of large raised stones

lines appear to lead us
along the hillside

bog tufts softening
beneath each step

bracken and briar
restraining our march

clawing us back, slowing
us to perception's pace.

II

A small animal halts,
starts, leaps away

and a lark begins
its dizzy, singing climb

towards the upper skies
and now another stone appears

ancient, looming, mossed
long ago placed,

lifted to be a signpost
along the old path.

III

Let us climb further.
As one thought leads
to another, so one lich-

ened snout of stone
still leads one on,
beckons to a final one.

IV

Under its raised slab
thin trickles of water

gather to a shallow pool
in which the head stone

mirrors, and rears
to regard its shadow self,

and a diligent spider weaves
a trembling, silver web

a skein of terrible delicacy
swaying to the wind's touch

a fragile, silken scarf
a veined translucent leaf.

V

This is the slope of loneliness.
This is the hill of silence.
This is the winds' fortress.
Our world's polestar.
A stony patience.

VI

We have reached a shelf
that surveys the valley

on these plains below
a battle flowed and ebbed

and the gored, spent warrior
was ferried up here

where water and herbs
might staunch his wounds.

VII

Let us also lay ourselves
down in this silence

let us also be healed
wounds closed, senses cleansed

as over our bowed heads
the mad larks multiply

needles stabbing the sky
in an ecstasy of stitching fury

against the blue void
while from clump and tuft

cranny and cleft, soft-footed
curious, the animals gather around.

3

# TIME IN ARMAGH

# 1

Heavy bells that rang above my head,
Sounds loneliness distilled
When Frank Lenny led me, gentle guide,
Under the Cathedral shade
And the gross carillon stirred.

Sick again, I had arrived months late
To hear the shoal's
Seashell roaring along the corridors
While my old neighbours
Fell silent in the cold parlour.

Garvaghey and Glencull were fleeing,
Leaving me to float,
A stray leaf, down the furious whirlpool
Of a junior seminary
From dawn Mass to Gaelic football.

Cowering at the dark soutane's swirl
Along the study hall;
Harder still, in the long dormitory's chill,
The midnight patrol
With probing torch, and cane's swish!

The holy war against the growing body
In the name of chastity,
As the Dean peers over my writing shoulder
Into my first diary:
'Any little girls' names there, have we?'

Would there have been a warm-breasted army!
Dear Frank Lenny,
For you, the flesh never raised a difficulty,
As you led us all
In solemn procession towards the Cathedral,

Satin-surpliced, with white gloves to uphold
The train of the cardinal.
Pageboy, Head Prefect, ordained priest,
Your path was straight:
One of their own, a natural for the episcopate.

Who would not envy such early certainty?
Across your celibate's bed
You fell last year, gone early upwards
Towards the heavens
Which, steadfast, you still believed in.

If, late again, I arrive flaunting my rival beliefs,
My secular life,
Will you be there, to greet and guide me,
White-gloved, gentle,
Proud of our Tyrone accent, my boyhood Virgil?

# 2

Then there were the terrible nights when Belfast was bomb
and planes of the Luftwaffe penetrated as far as Armagh. O
crossed low over the tossing trees at the end of the football fiel
we could hear the engine's roar as it swooped. Crouched in th
dampness of the hastily constructed air-raid shelters we awaite
the shudder, the flash, the quick moment of extinction.

'Oh, Lord,' I prayed, on my knees at the leaf-strewn entranc
'let me not feel death, only die so suddenly that I will not kno
what it is all about.'

The air seemed to quiver with the upward beat of wings
the plane zoomed over the school buildings and away, leavi
the frightened boys staring at the sky, the silvered spires of t
Cathedral; moonlit nights were best for bombing raids. In th
moment he had known everything; the possibility of death,
the shape of a dark angel, something apocalyptic and avengi
as the images conjured up in a Lenten sermon in the chap
Then the rising wail of the All Clear.

'It's gone. . . .'

In the candle- and torch-lit darkness of their concrete ca
the boys turned frightened heads upwards, no longer in fe
but in thanksgiving.

'It's gone', they chorused.

Father Rafferty, their favourite priest, blessed himself aga
and began to lead the Rosary, with relief, in the blessèd silen
of the raid's aftermath.

'Come now, boys, let us kneel down and pray to the Bless
Virgin, in thanks for having been saved, this time.'

As he knelt, running the beads through his fingers with pr
tised skill, he was aware of some menace, at the edge of
retina. From his vantage point he could see that, although t
themselves were safe and sound, the stain on the Eastern s
was growing, like a bloodshot eye.

'Let us pray,' he said to himself, 'for all the poor people
Belfast.'

# 3

Behind and above our bowed heads
At the end of the long study hall
Was a viewing window, a Judas hole,
To spy on the mischief we were up to;
Caherty acting the maggot as usual,
Montague or Muldoon gabbling,
John Donaghy studying racing form.
Once John and I made a stink bomb
(A test tube of sulphuric acid and iron)
Which swiftly cleared out that hated room.
One of the best experiments I have done:
Spying on people is obscene. Besides, alas,
The only opening left was our imagination,
Sulphurous laughter our only weapon.

# 4

EXTRA MURAL

*for William Smyth*

Once a week, the Sunday walk brought us back outside the walls, *extra muros*, in orderly formation. There was the Geography Walk, led by our most mild master, the Reverend Mickey Block. His real name, Rafferty, I remember with difficulty; we certainly thought he had a beam missing. He droned on happily about the drumlins that had formed Armagh, a scatter of little eggshaped hills deposited by the Ice Age: the two Cathedrals which confronted each other across the city were founded on drumlins. He might be daft on drumlins but he also doted on terminal moraines and river basins, like the Boyne, and loved to draw the loops of an oxbow, meanders created by rough ground which the insistent river slow-nudged. The Moy had an oxbow lake like the Mississippi which spelt aloud was a snake slithering, with a hiccup. Did anyone live in a townland with an esker? I put up my hand: Eskra was next door to Garvaghey.

Coniferous and deciduous trees clung to or lost their leaves in winter, stalactites and stalagmites fell from or rose to rooves

of caves, mountains pleated and buckled into synclines and
anticlines: the earth was a living theatre. Chosen pupils crept
across the lawn on an important mission every morning, to
consult the rain guage set in the grass near the Senior Wall
a step away from the trees. The water collected overnight was
measured in a graduated cylinder, and the results entered in
a logbook beside the barograph with its moving pen which
traced the line of pressure in millibars. Dear Mickey Block,
kept us amused and busy with his dreams: his stocky little figure
would stop before some rushy gap while he conjured up, with
oblivious eloquence, some lost glory that we could barely see.
Rumour (school's private waveband) had it that he was arrested
as a spy while pottering around during the Long Vac, making
sketches of areas used for Allied War manoeuvres. Anyway, at
the end of Second Year, he did not come back.

# 5

LUNATIC

*Screwy*, or *Nuts*, they called me,
Because of my hawk, or handsaw, stance.
I would treat nothing seriously
Where all was harsh, boorish, ignorant.
Sated with small cruelties, I soon learnt
To sing dumb, or pull a loony face;
An antic disposition, my best defence.
My best advance, to leap exams like hurdles
Towards the fabled world of films and girls.
Once I doffed my jester's cap and bells
To front a hunger-strike, a mute rebellion.
To see the Dean flinch was brief recompense,
The soon palling pleasure of the dark accomplice:
Good pupils, grown just as mean as them.

# 6

> *I, too, drew my hand back from the cane.*
> — Juvenal

I

*Hazing,* they call it in America,
but I already knew it from Armagh,
the fledgeling hauled to the pump,

protesting, by the bigger boys
to be baptised with his nickname,
*Froggy, Screwy, Rubberneck* or *Dopey,*

some shameful blemish, his least attract-
ive aspect, hauled out to harry, haunt him
through his snail years in St Patrick's,

a five-year sentence. Even in the chapel,
in that hush of prayers and incense
the same cruelty was ritually practised,

shoving the prongs of the dividers
into the thighs of the smaller boy
who knelt before you. He couldn't cry

in such a sacred atmosphere, disturb
the priest murmuring on the altar,
the tinkle for the lofted Eucharist.

Sometimes, they used a Sacred Heart pin
to jab the victim. Tears spilt down
his face, while the Blessed Virgin

smiled inside the altar rails, and
Christ stumbled from station to station
around our walls, to His crucifixion,

thorn spiked, our exemplary victim.

335

## II

Then there was the gym and Gaelic football,
both compulsory. Dopey hid down a manhole
to escape these Spartan training sessions

where his slower wits betrayed him
to more jibes and taunts. He held on
but thirty years later, a grown man,

he began to break down, a boy, weeping,
plunged in the pit again, long hours waiting
in that damp darkness, until he heard

the thud of studded boots above his head.

## III

Endless games designed to keep us pure —
'Keep your hands out of your pockets, boys' —
we wore togs even in the showers.

No wonder Donaghy fired a brick through
a window when he left. 'I loathed every hour,
every minute,' wrote Des from Bangor,

'what you learnt was to be a survivor.
Remember our eccentric English music master;
what you need is a jolly good six-ah!'

Which, gentle soul, he never administered.
But those of the order of Melchisedech
were no slouches when it came to the stick.

Father Roughan, all too rightly named,
had a fine selection of swishing canes,
test-lashing the air before he landed one

right down the middle of the open palm,
or tingling along the shaking fingertips,
until the hand was ridged with welts.

Dismissed, the boys tried to hide
and hug their hurt under the armpits,
not a whimper, until safely outside

where the cub pack huddled around them,
offering the cold comfort of admiration:
sudden conspiracy of bully and victim

united before the black-skirted enemy.
Our stiff upper lip was an Ulster clamp.
No whingeing. No quarter for the crybaby.

Still to this late day, I rage blind
whenever I hear that hectoring tone,
trying to put another human being down.

The guilt givers who know what is right,
they can shove their rules. A system
without love is a crock of shite.


# 7

WAITING

Halting in Dungannon between trains
We often wandered outside town
To see the camp where German
Prisoners were kept. A moist litter
Of woodshavings showed
Ground hastily cleared, and then —

The huge parallelogram
Of barbed wire, nakedly measured
And enclosed like a football field
With the guard towers rising, aloof
As goalposts, at either end.

Given length and breadth we knew
The surface area the prisoners paced
As one hung socks to dry outside
His Nissen hut, another tried
To hum and whistle 'Lili Marlene':
They seemed to us much the same

As other adults, except in their
Neutral dress, and finding it normal
To suffer our gaze, like animals,
As we squatted and pried, for an hour
Or more, about their human zoo

Before it was time for shopfronts,
Chugging train, Vincentian school.
A small incident, soon submerged
In our own brisk, bell-dominated rule:
Until, years later, I saw another camp —
Rudshofen, in the fragrant Vosges —

Similar, but with local improvements:
The stockade where they knelt the difficult,
The laboratory for minor experiments,
The crematorium for Jews and gypsies
Under four elegant pine towers, like minarets.

This low-pitched style seeks exactness,
Determined not to betray the event.
But as I write, the grid of barbed
Wire rises abruptly around me,
The smell of woodshavings plugs
My nostrils, a carrion stench.

# 8

I bribed Caherty with a Mars Bar
a day to replace me at the High Altar.
Our College oratory was being painted:
scaffoldings, buckets between the Stations
of the Cross, the canvas draped statues.
So we had been allotted the morning run
of Armagh Cathedral, and it was my turn
to mumble back the Latin responses.

Checked and choked by my stammer,
how could I serve our houseled Lord
in such *a halting, disagreeable manner*?
I recalled a funeral service at home,
every response dragging like a chain
till a weary priest took over: *humiliation.*

Dean Roughan spotted my weak trick,
summoned me to his study, canes racked
near the door, beneath a chilling text
in block letters: NO FUN LIKE WORK.
A Senior, I was offered the choice —
a public caning or to raise my voice
again next week, which would be High Mass.

The brisk Dean had forgotten that to sing,
albeit tunelessy, is possible to the stammering.
Father MacCurtain, who quavered *'Panis Angelicus'*
in his high tenor at our school concerts,
was the celebrant. Moon-faced old Mack
was a good sort, bending over the tabernacle,
then turning to smile sly encouragement
as we began to intone our formal chant.

Slowly, the whole school joined warmly in:
the high vault rang with grave Gregorian.

# 9

Our History Master was a curly-headed young priest ᴠ
leaned too close to us in class, the better to inspect
copybooks, *moryah*. Often I felt his downy cheek press aga
mine, though I doubt if he knew what he was doing: he wa
ignorant and naive as the rest of us. Yet he could be enthusia
in our first term, before the official N. I. Syllabus swallowed
we learnt about something called Early Irish Civilisatio
loved it, Larne flints, osiered banquet halls, the bronze trum
of Lough na Shade. *Then it was back to the Origins of the In*
*trial Revolution.*

Once myth and reality warmly met, when we swar
over Navan Fort. Sheep grazed where Cuchulainn and his ꜰ
King, Conor, argued, a quarry ate the grass where Deirdre
saw her young warrior. But we were doing English and Moc
History for our State exams, not Irish, so the mythic figᴜ
melted into the mizzling rain, the short views returned: we ᴠ
standing on a large green hillock in the County Armagh, No
ern Ireland, not on the magic mound of Emain Macha,
hillfort of the Red Branch knights. *There would surely be a q*
*tion on William Pitt, and the Corn Laws.*

History Walks were rarer than Geography, perhaps bec
they feared to disturb our local nest of pismires. History
about us in our infancy, with many levels, but only one stra
open. They did not have to explain to us why our new Cathe
had been built on a higher hill. We explored our ancient ᴜ
when we ran footloose through town. We marvelled at its ec
ing emptiness, the rotting flags of Imperial wars. The roll ca
the side chapel of the Royal Irish Fusiliers might have taugʜ
something; O's and Macs mingled in death with good Prc
names, Hamilton, Hewitt, Taylor, Acheson.

Instead we ran down the curling, cobbled hill, giggling ᴠ
guilt. Doomed as any Armada, the lost city of Ard Macha cc
in upon itself, whorl upon whorl, a broken aconite. Layer u
layer had gone to its making, from Cuchulainn to St Patᵣ
from fleet-footed Macha to Primate Robinson's gaggle of G
gian architects. But the elegance of the Mall was of no ᵃ
against simpleminded sectarianism; Armagh, a maimed c
tal, a damaged pearl.

We sensed this as we sifted through the shards in the

County Museum. Bustled around the glass cases by Curly Top, we halted before a Yeoman's coat, alerted by our party song, 'The Croppy Boy'. And we read about the battle of Diamond Hill between 'Peep-o'-Day Boys' and Catholic Defenders which led to the founding of the Orange Order at Loughgall, a canker among the apple blossoms.

We did not discuss this in our History Class, which now dealt with the origins of the First World War, from the shot in Sarajevo. It did crop up in R. K., Religious Knowledge, where the Dean warned us against the dangers of Freemasonry. A Catholic could never become King of England or President of the United States; everywhere the black face of Protestantism barred the way to good Catholic boys. Amongst the cannon on the Mall the Protestant boys played cricket, or kicked a queer shaped ball like a pear. According to my Falls Road pal Protestant balls bounced crooked as the Protestants themselves. One day that banter would stop when a shot rang out on the Cathedral Road.

# 10

ABSENCE

One by one, the small boys nod off.
The only light left, my Prefect's torch.
For an hour I have patrolled the dorm,
Checking that Romeo Forte is not snoring,
That Gubby Lenny is not homesick, weeping,
The terrible O'Neill twins not whispering.
Surely Dean Roughan will not do the rounds
Tonight, so I have a chance to warm up again
My letter to a convent girl in Lurgan,
Concealed inside my Modern History volume.
*I can still smell the fragrance of your hair,*
*Your small ears, like seashells,* and so on.
The water pipes knock, the great bells sound.
To the chill dark of my cubicle I summon
The sweet blessing of a girlish presence,
Shaping my lips to kiss her absence.

## 11

A WELCOMING PARTY

*Wie war das möglich?*

That final newsreel of the war:
A welcoming party of almost shades
Met us at the cinema door
Clicking what remained of their heels.

From nests of bodies like hatching eggs
Flickered insectlike hands and legs
And rose an ululation, terrible, shy;
Children conjugating the verb 'to die'.

One clamoured mutely of love
From a mouth like a burnt glove;
Others upheld hands bleak as begging bowls
Claiming the small change of our souls.

Some smiled at us as protectors.
Can those bones live?
Our parochial brand of innocence
Was all we had to give.

To be always at the periphery of incident
Gave my childhood its Irish dimension; drama of unevent:
Yet doves of mercy, as doves of air,
Can falter here as anywhere.

That long dead Sunday in Armagh
I learnt one meaning of total war
And went home to my Christian school
To belt a football through the air.

# 12

Armagh. Its calm Georgian Mall.
A student's memory of bells, the carillon
echoing from the new Cathedral, glooms
over the old walls and sleeping cannon,
the incongruously handsome Women's Prison.
By the railings, two impassive R.U.C. men.
I ring formally and ask for Bernadette:
an incredulous giggle and a slammed door
is the iron answer that I get.

Exposed on the steps like Seanchan,
I intone the scop stresses of my Derry poem.
*Lines of suffering/lines of defeat.*
One of the constables shifts his feet,
the other is grinning broadly. A secret
acolyte of poetry? I can hear him
rubbing his hands in the guardroom;
'Boys, that was great crack! The Fenians
must be losing. This time they sent a lunatic.'

# 13

Cathedral,
I shape you in the air with my hands,
On a night when a cutting wind
Counts the hours
With chill bursts of rain.

Cathedral,
Tall-spired guardian of my childhood
In the Ulster night,
Over Saint Patrick's city
The roofs are eyelashed with rain

As the iron bell
Swings out again, each quarter's notes
Dwindling down a shaft of past
And present, to drown
In that throat of stone.

I lived in Armagh in a time of war,
The least conscious time of my life.
Between two stones may lie
My future self
Waiting that you pass by.

If she pass by,
Dislodging the stone of my youth,
Cathedral,
Enclosure and cloister, prow of lost surety,
Resound for me!

# BORDER SICK CALL

FOR SEAMUS MONTAGUE, MD, MY BROTHER,
in memory of a journey in winter
along the Fermanagh-Donegal border.

*Looks like, I'm breaking the ice!* — Fats Waller

*Weary, God!*
*of starfall and snowfall,*
*weary of north winter, and weary*
*of myself like this, so cold and thoughtful.*
— Hayden Carruth

**1**

Hereabouts, signs are obliterated,
but habit holds.

We wave a friendly goodbye
to a Customs Post that has twice
leaped into the air
to come to earth again
as a makeshift, a battered trailer
hastily daubed green: *An Stad.*

The personnel still smile
and wave back,
their limbs still intact.

Fragments of reinforced concrete,
of zinc, timber, sag and glint in the hedge
above them, the roof and walls
of their old working place:

> *Long years in France,*
> *I have seen little like this,*
> mème dans le guerre Algerienne,
> *the impossible as normal,*
> *lunacy made local,*
> *surrealism made risk.*

Along the glistening main road
snow plough-scraped, salt-sprinkled,
we sail, chains clanking,
the surface bright, hard, treacherous
with only one slow, sideways skid
before we reach the side road.

Along ruts ridged with ice
the car now rocks, until we reach
a gap walled with snow where
silent folk wait and watch
for our, for your, arrival.

The high body of a tractor
rides us a few extra yards

on its caterpillar wheels
till it also slips and slopes
into a hidden ditch
to tilt helpless, one large
welted tyre spinning.


## 2


Shanks' mare now, it seems,
for the middle-aged,
marching between hedges
burdened with snow,
low bending branches
which sigh to the ground
as we pass, to spring back.

And the figures fall back
with soft murmurs of
'on the way home, doctor?'
shades that disappear
to merge into the fields,
their separate holdings.

Only you seem to know
where you are going
as we march side by side,
following the hillslope
whose small crest shines
like a pillar of salt,
only the so solid scrunch
and creak of snow crystals
thick-packed underneath
your fur boots, my high
farmer's wellingtons.

Briefly we follow
the chuckling rush
of a well-fed stream
that swallows, and swells
with the still-melting snow
until it loses itself
in a lough, a mountain tarn
filmed with crisp ice

which now flashes sunlight,
a mirror of brightness,
reflecting, refracting
a memory, a mystery:

> Misty afternoons in winter
> we climb to a bog pool;
> rushes fossilised in ice.
> A run up, and a slide —
> boots score a glittering
> path, until a heel slips
> and a body measures its length
> slowly on ice, starred with
> cracks like an old plate.

Into this wide, white world
we climb slowly higher,
no tree, or standing stone,
only cold sun and moorland,
where a stray animal,
huddled, is a dramatic event,
a gate a silvered statement,
its bars burred with frost,
tracks to a drinking trough,
rutted hard as cement:
a silent, islanded cottage,
its thatch slumped in,
windows cracked, through which,
instead of Christians, cattle
peer out, in dumb desolation.

> And I remember how, in Fintona,
> you devoured Dante by the fireside,
> a small black World's Classic.
> But no purgatorial journey
> reads stranger than this,
> our Ulster border pilgrimage
> where demarcations disappear,
> landmarks, forms, and farms vanish
> into the ultimate coldness of an ice age,
> as we march towards Lettercran,
> in steelblue, shadowless light,
> The Ridge of the Tree, the heart of whiteness.

348

# 3

We might be astronauts creak-
ing over the cold curve
of the moon's surface, as our boots
sink, rasp over crusted snow,
sluggish, thick, dreamlike,

until, for the first time
in half-an-hour, we see
a human figure, shrunken
but agile, an old, old man
bending over something, poking
at it furiously with a stick:
carcass of fox or badger?

'Hello,' we hallo, like strangers
on an Antarctic or arctic ice floe —
Amunsen greeting a penguin! —
each detail in cold relief.

Hearing us, the small figure halts,
turns an unbelieving face, then
takes off, like a rabbit or hare
with a wounded leg, the stick its pivot,
as it hirples along, vigorously
in the wrong, the opposite
direction, away from us,
the stricken gait of the aged
transformed into a hobble,
intent as a lamplighter.

We watch as our pathfinder,
our potential guide, dwindles
down the valley, steadily
diminishing until
he burrows,
bolts under,
disappears into,
a grove of trees.

'And who might that be,
would you say?' I ask my brother
as we plod after him
at half his pace. 'Surely
one of my most urgent patients,'
he says, with a wry smile,
'the sick husband gone to get
his sicker wife back to bed
before I arrive.' And he smiles
again, resignedly.

'And besides, he wants to tidy
the place up, before the Doctor
comes. Things will be grand
when we finally get there:
he just wasn't expecting anyone
to brave the storm.

'But there'll be a good welcome
when we come.'

And sure enough all is waiting,
shining, inside the small cottage.
The fire laughs on the hearth,
bellows flared, whilst the dog rises
to growl, slink, then wag its tail.

# 4

My brother is led into the bedroom.
Then himself, a large-eared, blue-eyed gnome,
still pert with the weight of his eighty years,
discourses with me before his hearth,
considerately, like a true host.

'Border, did you say,
how many miles to the border?
Sure we don't know where it starts
or ends up here, except we're lost
unless the doctor or postman finds us.

'But we didn't always complain.
Great hills for smuggling they were,
I made a packet in the old days,
when the big wars were rumbling on,
before this auld religious thing came in.

'You could run a whole herd through
between night and morning, and no one
the wiser, bar the B-Specials,
and we knew every mother's son
well enough to grease the palm,
quietlike, if you know what I mean.
Border be damned, it was a godsend.
Have you ever noticed, cows have no religion?'

*Surefooted, in darkness,*
*stick-guiding his animals,*
*in defiance of human frontiers,*
*the oldest of Irish traditions,*
*the* creach *or cattle raid,*
*as old as the* Táin.

Now, delighted with an audience,
my host rambles warmly on;
holding forth on his own hearth:

'Time was, there'd be a drop
of the good stuff in the house,'
the head cocked sideways
before he chances a smile,
'but not all is gone.
Put your hand in the thatch
there, left of the door,
and see what you find.'

Snug as an egg under a hen,
a small prescription bottle of colourless poteen.
'Take that medicine with you for the road home.
You were brave men to come.'

# 5

Downhill, indeed, is easier,
while there is still strong light,
an eerie late afternoon glow
boosted by the sullen weight
of snow on the hedges,
still or bowing to the ground
again, as we pass, an iceblue
whiteness beneath our steady tread;
a snow flurry, brief, diamond-hard,
under a frieze of horsetail cloud.

The same details of field, farm
unravelling once again, as the doctor
plods on, incongruous in his fur boots
(but goodness often looks out of place),
downhill, with the same persistence
in a setting as desolate as if
a glacier had just pushed off:

> *Thick and vertical*
> *the glacier slowly*
> *a green white wall*
> *grinding mountains*
> *scooping hollows*
> *a gross carapace*
> *sliding down the*
> *face of Europe*
> *to seep, to sink*
> *its melting weight*
> *into chilly seas;*
> *bequeathing us*
> *ridges of stone,*
> *rubble of gravel,*
> *eskers of hardness:*
> *always within us —*
> *a memory of coldness.*

Only one detail glints different.
On that lough, where the sun burns
above the silver ice, like a calcined stone,
a chilling fire, orange red,
a rowboat rests, chained in ice,
ice at gunwhale, prow and stern,
ice jagged on the anchor ropes;
still, frozen, 'the small bark of my wit',
*la navicella del mio ingegno.*
Why could I not see it on the way
up, only on the journey home,

I wonder as my brother briefly disappears
across the half-door of another house,
leaving me to wait, as glimmers gather
into the metallic blues of twilight,
and watch, as if an inward eye were opening,
details expand in stereoscopic brightness,
a buck hare, not trembling, unabashed,
before he bounds through the frozen grass,
a quick scatter of rabbits, while
a crow clatters to the lower wood,
above the incessant cries of the sheep herd.


# 6

When my brother returns, breath pluming,
although he risks only a swallow,
the fiery drink unleashes his tongue:
from taciturn to near-vision,

'I heard you chatting to old MacGurren,
but the real border is not between
countries, but between life and death,
that's where the doctor comes in.

'I have sat beside old and young
on their death beds, and have seen
the whole house waiting, as for birth,
everything scoured, spick-and-span,
footsteps tiptoeing around.

'But the pain is endless,
you'd think no one could endure it,
but still they resist, taste the respite,
until the rack tightens again
on the soiled, exhausted victim.'

*But the poem is endless,*
*the poem is strong as our weakness,*
*strong in its weakness,*
*it will never cease until it has said*
*what cannot be said.*

*The sighs and crying of someone*
*who is leaving this world*
*in all its solid, homely detail*
*for another they have only heard tell of,*
*in the hearsay called religion,*
*or glimpsed uneasily in dream.*

'People don't speak of it,
lacking a language for this terrible thing,
a forbidden subject, a daily happening,
pushed aside until it comes in.

I remember the first time I saw it
on my first post as a *locum*.'

(That smell in the sickroom —
stale urine and *faeces* —
the old man on the grey bed,
his wife crouched in darkness.

Many generations of family
lined up along the stairs
and out into the farmyard:
the youngest barely aware

of the drama happening inside
that unblinking frame of light;
but horseplaying, out loud.
Three generations, and the tree shaking.

He has lain still for months
but now his muscles tighten,
he lifts himself into a last
bout of prayers and imprecations.

The old woman also starts up
but there is no recognition,
only that ultimate effort, before
he falls back, broken,

The rosary lacing stiff fingers.
'I did not expect to witness
the process in such a rush:
it still happens in these lost places.')


# 7

Just as we think we are finally clear,
another shade steps out from the shadows
(out of the darkness, they gather to your goodness),
with its ritual murmured demand:
'Doctor, would you be so good to come in?
The wife is taken bad again.'

All the clichés of rural comedy
(which might be a rural tragedy),
as he leads us along a tangled path,
our clabbery *via smaritta*.

Briars tug at us, thorn and whin
jag us, we trudge along a squelching drain;
my brother and I land ankle-deep in slush,
a gap guttery as a boghole,
and he has to haul us out by hand,
abjectly, 'Sorry we've no back lane.'

In his house, where an Aladdin burns,
we step out of our boots, socks,
before the warm bulk of the Rayburn,
and my brother pads, barefooted,
into the back room, where a woman moans.

Nursing a mug of tea in the kitchen
I confer anxiously with her cowed man.
'She's never been right since the last wain,
God knows, it's hard on the women.'

Three ragged little ones in wellingtons
stare at the man from Mars,
suck their thumbs and say nothing.
There is a tinny radio but no television.
A slight steam rises where our socks hang.
At last my brother beckons him in.

When we leave, no more conversation;
the labourer stumbling before us,
his hand shielding a candle
which throws a guttering flame:
a sheltering darkness of firs, then,
spiked with icicles, a leafless thorn,
where the gate scringes on its stone.

When we stride again on the road,
there is a bright crop of stars,
the high, clear stars of winter,
the studded belt of Orion,
and a silent, frost-bright moon
upon snow crisp as linen
spread on death or bridal bed;
blue tinged as a spill of new
milk from the crock's lip.

# 8

Another mile, our journey is done.
The main road again. The snow-laden car
gleams strange as a space machine.

We thrust snow from the roof;
sit cocooned as the engine warms,
and the wipers work their crescents clean

With a beat steady as a metronome.
Brother, how little we know of each other!
Driving from one slaughter to another

Once, you turned on the car radio
to hear the gorgeous pounding rhythms
of your first symphony: Beethoven.

The hair on your nape crawled.
Startled by the joy, the energy,
the answering surge in your own body.

In the face of suffering, unexpected affirmation.
For hours we've been adrift from humankind,
navigating our bark in a white landlocked ocean.

Will a stubborn devotion suffice,
sustained by an ideal of service?
Will dogged goodwill solve anything?

Headlights carve a path through darkness
back through Pettigo, towards Enniskillen.
The customs officials wave us past again.

But in what country have we been?

# EDITORS' NOTE

*Collected Poems* gathers most of the contents of John Montague's principal collections: *Forms of Exile* (1958), *Poisoned Land and Other Poems* (1961), *A Chosen Light* (1967), *Tides* (1970), *The Rough Field* (1972), *A Slow Dance* (1976), *The Great Cloak* (1978), *The Dead Kingdom* (1984), *Mount Eagle* (1988), and *Time in Armagh* (1993). Some of the poems have been revised. A few translations from the Irish, originally published in *A Fair House* (1973), are also included. (For a more complete record of the author's publications, see Thomas Dillon Redshaw's bibliography in the *Irish University Review*, 19:1 (Spring 1989).

Consistent with the author's carefully composed sequences, which in part recover and present in new light poems from earlier volumes, we have inaugurated *Collected Poems* with his three major 'orchestrations' which thereby strike the notes of his enduring themes and concerns: his family's and Ulster's history (*The Rough Field*), his attention to love through an investigation of a marriage, its dissolution and aftermath (*The Great Cloak*), and his *dinnseanchas* or place wisdom, evoked by a journey northwards through the troubled landscape of his youth (*The Dead Kingdom*).

These sustained movements are followed by the lyrics which show both the poet's development and the range of his gift. *Collected Poems* then concludes with two more-recent sequences, *Time in Armag*h and the uncollected *Border Sick Call* which, with characteristic sweep, both remember and take stock of a familiar civilization.

This arrangement reflects the pattern of his life's work so far: part self-portrait, it is even more a 'landscape with figures' — and it has the look of a masterpiece.

Peter Fallon / Dillon Johnston

# INDEX OF TITLES

361

363

# INDEX OF FIRST LINES

369

375